The Quadroon; Or, a Lover's Adventures in Louisiana - Primary Source Edition

Mayne Reid

Nabu Public Domain Reprints:

You are holding a reproduction of an original work published before 1923 that is in the public domain in the United States of America, and possibly other countries. You may freely copy and distribute this work as no entity (individual or corporate) has a copyright on the body of the work. This book may contain prior copyright references, and library stamps (as most of these works were scanned from library copies). These have been scanned and retained as part of the historical artifact.

This book may have occasional imperfections such as missing or blurred pages, poor pictures, errant marks, etc. that were either part of the original artifact, or were introduced by the scanning process. We believe this work is culturally important, and despite the imperfections, have elected to bring it back into print as part of our continuing commitment to the preservation of printed works worldwide. We appreciate your understanding of the imperfections in the preservation process, and hope you enjoy this valuable book.

THE QUADROON;

OR,

A LOVER'S ADVENTURES IN LOUISIANA.

BY

CAPTAIN MAYNE REID,

AUTHOR OF "THE SCALP-HUNTERS."

IN THREE VOLUMES.

VOL. III.

LONDON:

GEORGE W. HYDE, 13 PATERNOSTER ROW.

1856.

[*Right of Translation reserved by the Author.*]

THE QUADROON.

CHAPTER I.

THE WATCH AND RING.

I ROSE from my seat, and turned towards D'Hauteville with a glance of despair. I needed not to tell him the result. My look would have announced it, but he had been gazing over my shoulder and knew all.

"Shall we go, Monsieur?" I asked.

"Not yet—stay a moment," replied he, placing his hand upon my arm.

"And why?" I asked; "I have not a dollar. I have lost all. I might have known it would be so. Why stay here, sir?"

I spoke somewhat brusquely. I confess, I was at the moment in anything but an amiable mood. In addition to my prospects for the morrow, a suspicion had flashed across my mind that my new friend was not loyal. His knowledge of these men—his having counselled me to play there—the accident, to say the least, a strange one, of our again meeting with the "sportsmen" of the boat, and under such a new phase—the great celerity with which my purse had been "cleared out,"—all these circumstances passing rapidly through my mind, led me naturally enough to suspect D'Hauteville of treason. I ran rapidly over our late conversation. I tried to remember whether he had said or done anything to guide me into this particular hell. Certainly he had not proposed my playing, but rather opposed it; and I could not remember that by word or act he had endeavoured to introduce me to the game. Moreover, he seemed as much astonished as myself at seeing these gentlemen behind the table.

What of all that? The surprise might have been well feigned. Possibly enough; and, after my late experience of the pork-merchant, probably enough, Monsieur D'Hauteville was also a partner in the firm of Chorley, Hatcher, and Co. I wheeled round with an angry expression on my lips, when the current of my thoughts was suddenly checked, and turned into a new channel. The young Creole stood looking up in my face—he was not so tall as I—gazing upon me out of his beautiful eyes, and waiting until my moment of abstraction should pass. Something glittered in his outstretched hand. It was a purse. I could see the yellow coins shining through the silken network. It was a purse of gold!

"Take it!" he said, in his soft silvery voice.

My heart fell abashed within me. I could scarce stammer forth a reply. Had he but known my latest thoughts, he might have been able to read the flush of shame that so suddenly mantled my cheeks.

"No, Monsieur," I replied, "this is too generous of you. I cannot accept it."

"Come—come! Why not? Take it, I pray—try fortune again. She has frowned on you of late, but remember she is a fickle goddess—and may yet smile on you. Take the purse, man!"

"Indeed, Monsieur, I cannot after what I—pardon me—if you knew——"

"Then must *I* play for you—remember the purpose that brought us here! Remember Aurore!"

"Oh!"

This ejaculation, wrung from my heart, was the only answer I could make, before the young Creole had turned to the faro-table, and was placing his gold upon the cards.

I stood watching him with feelings of astonishment and admiration, mingled with anxiety for the result.

What small white hands! What a brilliant jewel, sparkling on his finger—a diamond! It has caught the eyes of the players, who gloat upon it as it passes back and forward to the cards. Chorley and Hatcher have both noticed it. I saw them exchange their peculiar glance as they did so. Both are polite to him. By the large bets he is laying he has won their esteem. Their attention in calling out the card when he wins, and in handing him his cheques, is marked and assiduous. He is the favoured bettor of the ring; and oh! how the eyes of those fair lemans gleam upon him with their wild and wicked meaning! Not one of them that would not love him for that sparkling gem!

I stood on one side watching with great anxiety—greater than if the stake had been my own. But it *was* my own. It was *for me*. The generous youth was playing away his gold for *me*.

My suspense was not likely to be of long duration. He was losing rapidly,—recklessly losing. He had taken my place at the table, and along with it my ill-luck. Almost every bet he made was "raked" into the bank, until his last coin lay upon the cards. Another turn, and that, too, chinked as it fell into the cash-box of the croupier!

"Come now, D'Hauteville! Come away!" I whispered, leaning over, and laying hold of his arm.

"How much against this?" he asked the banker, without heeding me—"how much, sir?"

As he put the question, he raised the gold guard over his head, at the same time drawing forth his watch.

I suspected this was his intention when

I first spoke. I repeated my request in a tone of entreaty—all in vain. He pressed Chorley for a reply.

The latter was not the man to waste words at such a crisis.

"A hundred dollars," said he, "for the watch—fifty more upon the chain."

"Beautiful!" exclaimed one of the players.

"They're worth more," muttered another.

Even in the *blazé* hearts around that table there were human feelings. There is always a touch of sympathy for him who loses boldly; and an expression of this in favour of the Creole youth could be heard, from time to time, as his money parted from him.

"Yes, that watch and chain are worth more," said a tall dark-whiskered man, who sat near the end of the table. This remark was made in a firm confident tone of voice, that seemed to command Chorley's attention.

"I'll look at it again, if you please?" said he, stretching across the table to D'Hauteville, who still held the watch in his hand.

The latter surrendered it once more to the gambler, who opened the case, and commenced inspecting the interior. It was an elegant watch, and chain also—of the fashion usually worn by ladies. They *were* worth more than Chorley had offered—though that did not appear to be the opinion of the pork-merchant.

"It's a good pile o' money, is a hundred an' fifty dollars," drawled he; "a good biggish pile, I reckon. I don't know much about such fixins meself, but it's full valley for that ar watch an' chain, I shed say."

"Nonsense!" cried several; "two hundred dollars—it's worth it all. See the jewels!"

Chorley cut short the discussion.

"Well," said he, "I don't think it worth

more than what I've bid, sir. But since you wish to get back what you've already lost, I don't mind staking two hundred against watch and chain together. Does that satisfy you?"

"Play on!" was the only answer made by the impatient Creole, as he took back his watch, and laid it down upon one of the cards.

It was a cheap watch to Chorley. It cost him but the drawing out of half-a-dozen cards, and it became his!

"How much against this?"

D'Hauteville drew off his ring, and held it before the dazzled eyes of the dealer.

At this crisis I once more interfered, but my remonstrance was unheeded. It was of no use trying to stay the fiery spirit of the Creole.

The ring was a diamond, or rather a collection of diamonds in a gold setting. It, like the watch, was also of the fashion worn by ladies; and I could hear some chader white fingers, and laid it on the centre of the card. It was the only bet made. The other players had become so interested in the result, that they withheld their stakes in order to watch it.

Chorley commenced drawing the cards. Each one as it came forth caused a momentary thrill of expectancy; and when aces, deuces, or trés with their broad white margins appeared outside the edge of that mysterious box, the excitement became intense.

It was a long time before two aces came together. It seemed as if the very importance of the stakes called for more than the usual time to decide the bet.

It was decided at length. The ring followed the watch!

I caught D'Hauteville by the arm, and drew him away from the table. This time he followed me unresistingly—as he had nothing more to lay.

"What matters it?" said he, with a gay air as we passed together out of the saloon. "Ah! yes—" he continued, changing his tone, "ah, yes, it does matter! It matters to *you*, and *Aurore!*"

CHAPTER II.

MY FORLORN HOPE.

It was pleasant escaping from that hot hell into the cool night air—into the soft light of a Southern moon. It would have been pleasant under other circumstances; but then the sweetest clime and loveliest scene would have made no impression upon me.

My companion seemed to share my bitterness of soul. His words of consolation were not without their influence; I knew they were the expressions of a real sympathy. His acts had already proved it.

It was, indeed, a lovely night. The white moon rode buoyantly through fleecy clouds, that thinly dappled the azure sky of Louisiana, and a soft breeze played through the now silent streets. A lovely night—

too sweet and balmy. My spirit would have preferred a storm. Oh! for black clouds, red lightning, and thunder rolling and crashing through the sky. Oh! for the whistling wind, and the quick pattering of the rain-drops. Oh! for a hurricane without, consonant to the storm that was raging within me!

It was but a few steps to the hotel; but we did not stop there. We could think better in the open air, and converse as well. Sleep had no charms for me, and my companion seemed to share my impulses; so passing once more from among the houses, we kept on towards the Swamp, caring not whither we went.

We walked side by side for some time without exchanging speech. Our thoughts were running upon the same theme,—the business of to-morrow. To-morrow no longer, for the tolling of the great cathedral clock had just announced the hour of midnight. In twelve hours more the *vente de l'ençan* would commence—in twelve hours more, they would be bidding for my betrothed!

Our steps were towards the "Shell Road," and soon our feet crunched upon the fragments of unios and bivalves that strewed the path. Here was a scene more in unison with our thoughts. Above and around waved the dark solemn cypress-trees, fit emblems of grief—rendered doubly lugubrious in their expression by the hoary *tillandsia*, that draped them like a couch of the dead. The sounds, too, that here saluted our ears had a soothing effect; the melancholy "coo-whoo-a" of the swamp-owl—the creaking chirp of the tree-crickets and cicadas—the solemn "tong-tong" of the bell-frog—the hoarse trumpet note of the greater batrachian—and high overhead the wild treble of the bull-bat, all mingled together in a concert, that, however disagreeable under other circumstances, now fell upon my ears like music, and even imparted a kind of sad pleasure to my soul.

And yet it was not my darkest hour. A darker was yet in store for me. Despite the very hopelessness of the prospect, I still clung to hope. A vague feeling it was; but it sustained me against despair. The trunk of a taxodium lay prostrate by the side of our path. Upon this we sat down.

We had exchanged scarce a dozen words since emerging from the hell. I was busy with thoughts of the morrow: my young companion, whom I now regarded in the light of an old and tried friend, was thinking of the same.

What generosity towards a stranger! what self-sacrifice! *Ah! little did I then know of the vast extent—the noble grandeur of that sacrifice!*

"There now remains but one chance," I said; "the chance that to-morrow's mail, or rather to-day's, may bring my letter. It might still arrive in time; the mail is due by ten o'clock in the morning."

"True," replied my companion, seemingly too busy with his own thoughts to give much heed to what I had said.

"If not," I continued, "then there is only the hope that he who shall become the purchaser, may afterwards sell her to *me*. I care not at what price, if I ——"

"Ah!" interrupted D'Hauteville, suddenly waking from his reverie; "it is just that which troubles me — that is exactly what I have been thinking upon. I fear, Monsieur, I fear ——"

"Speak on!"

"I fear there is no hope that he who buys her will be willing to sell her again."

"And why? Will not a large sum—— ?"

"No—no—I fear that he who buys will not give her up again, *at any price*."

"Ha! Why do you think so, M. D'Hauteville."

"I have my suspicion that a certain individual designs ——"

"Who?"

"M. Dominique Gayarre."

"Oh! heavens! Gayarre! Gayarre!"

"Yes; from what you have told me—from what I know myself—for I, too, have some knowledge of Dominique Gayarre."

"Gayarre! Gayarre! Oh, God!"

I could only ejaculate. The announcement had almost deprived me of the power of speech. A sensation of numbness seemed to creep over me—a prostration of spirit, as if some horrid danger was impending and nigh, and I without the power to avert it.

Strange this thought had not occurred to me before. I had supposed that the quadroon would be sold to some buyer in the ordinary course; some one who would be disposed to *resell* at a profit—perhaps an enormous one; but in time I should be prepared for that. Strange I had never thought of Gayarre becoming the purchaser. But, indeed, since the hour when I first heard of the bankruptcy, my thoughts had been running too wildly to permit me to reflect calmly upon anything.

Now it was clear. It was no longer a conjecture; most certainly, Gayarre would become the master of Aurore. Ere another night her body would be his property. Her soul——Oh, God! Am I awake?—do I dream?

"I had a suspicion of this before," continued D'Hauteville; "for I may tell you I know something of this family history—of Eugénie Besançon—of Aurore—of Gayarre the avocat. I had a suspicion before that Gayarre might desire to be the owner of Aurore. But now that you have told me of the scene in the dining-room, I no longer doubt this villain's design. Oh! it is infamous.

"Still further proof of it," continued D'Hauteville. "There was a man on the boat—you did not notice him, perhaps—an agent for Gayarre in such matters. A negro-

done to save her from this fearful man? to save me ——"

"It is of that I am thinking, and have been for the last hour. Be of good cheer, Monsieur! all hope is not lost. There is still one chance of saving Aurore. There is one hope left. Alas! I have known the time,—I, too, have been unfortunate — sadly—sadly—unfortunate. No matter now. We shall not talk of my sorrows, till yours have been relieved. Perhaps, at some future time you may know me, and my griefs—no more of that now. There is still one chance for Aurore, and she and you—both—may yet be happy. It must be so; I am resolved upon it. 'Twill be a wild act; but it is a wild story. Enough—I have no time to spare—I must be gone. Now to your hotel!—go and rest. To-morrow at twelve I shall be with you — at twelve in the Rotundo. Good night! Adieu!"

Without allowing me time to ask for an explanation, or make any reply, the Creole parted from me; and, plunging into a narrow street, soon passed out of sight!

Pondering over his incoherent words—over his unintelligible promise—upon his strange looks and manner,—I walked slowly to my hotel.

Without undressing I flung myself on my bed,—without a thought of going to sleep.

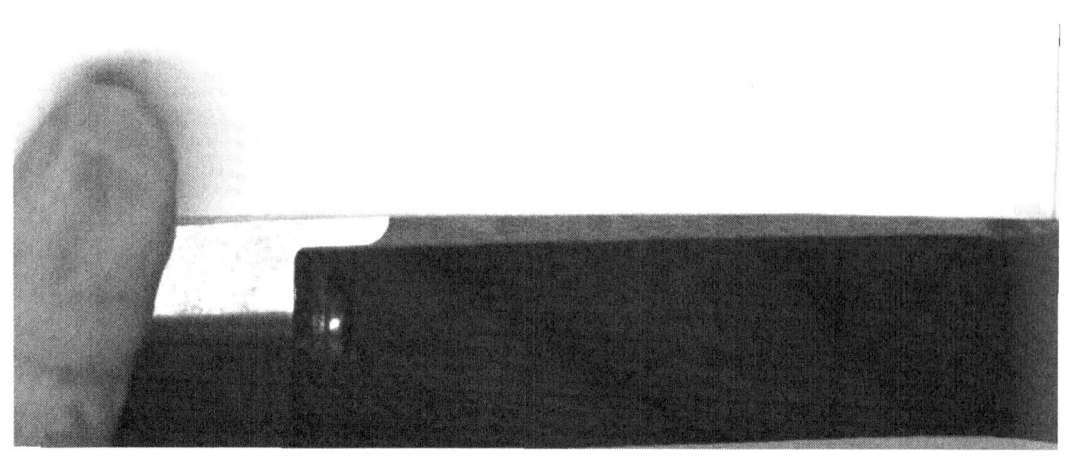

CHAPTER III.

THE ROTUNDO.

The thousand and one reflections of a sleepless night—the thousand and one alternations of hope, and doubt, and fear—the theoretic tentation of a hundred projects—all passed before my waking spirit. Yet when morning came, and the yellow sunlight fell painfully on my eyes, I had advanced no farther in any plan of proceeding. All my hopes centred upon D'Hauteville—for I no longer dwelt upon the chances of the mail.

To be assured upon this head, however, as soon as it had arrived, I once more sought the banking-house of Brown and Co. The negative answer to my inquiry was no longer a disappointment. I had anticipated it. When did money ever arrive in time for a crisis? Slowly roll the golden circles—slowly are they passed from hand to hand, and reluctantly parted with. This supply was due by the ordinary course of the mail; yet those friends at home, into whose executive hands I had entrusted my affairs, had made some cause of delay.

Never trust your business affairs to a *friend*. Never trust to a day for receiving a letter of credit, if to a friend belongs the duty of sending it. So swore I, as I parted from the banking-house of Brown and Co.

It was twelve o'clock when I returned to the Rue St. Louis. I did not re-enter the hotel—I walked direct to the *Rotundo*.

My pen fails to paint the dark emotions of my soul, as I stepped under the shadow of that spacious dome. I remember no feeling akin to what I experienced at that moment.

I have stood under the vaulted roof of the grand cathedral, and felt the solemnity

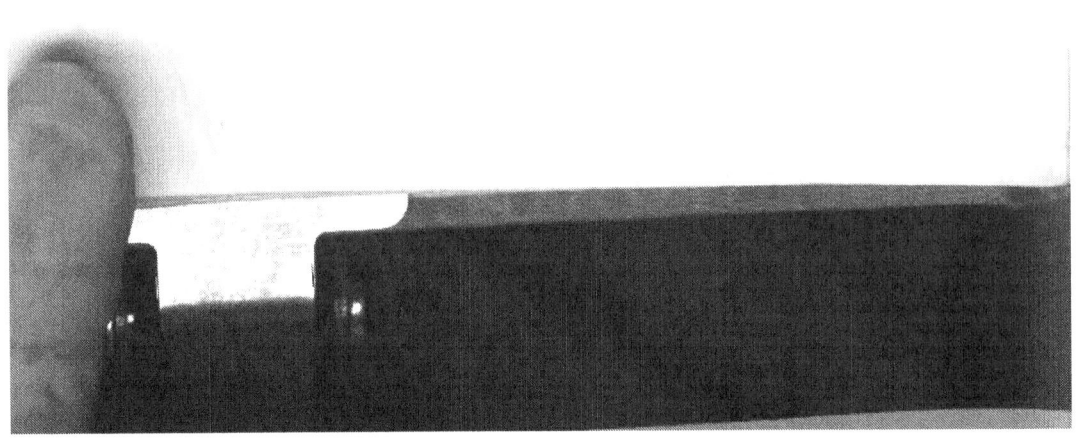

of religious awe—I have passed through the gilded saloons of a regal palace, that inspired me with pity and contempt—pity for the slaves who had sweated for that gilding, and contempt for the sycophants who surrounded me—I have inspected the sombre cells of a prison with feelings of pain—but I remembered no scene that had so painfully impressed me as that which now presented itself before my eyes.

Not sacred was that spot. On the contrary, I stood upon *desecrated* ground—desecrated by acts of the deepest infamy. This was the famed *slave-market of New Orleans*—the place where human bodies—I might almost say *human souls*—were bought and sold!

Many a forced and painful parting had these walls witnessed. Oft had the husband been here severed from his wife — the mother from her child. Oft had the bitter tear bedewed that marble pavement—

oft had that vaulted dome echoed back the sigh—nay more—the cry of the anguished heart!

I repeat it—my soul was filled with dark emotions as I entered within the precincts of that spacious hall. And no wonder—with such thoughts in my heart, and such a scene before my eyes, as I then looked upon.

You will expect a description of that scene. I must disappoint you. I cannot give one. Had I been there as an ordinary spectator—a reporter cool and unmoved by what was passing—I might have noted the details, and set them before you. But the case was far otherwise. One thought alone was in my mind—my eyes sought for one sole object—and that prevented me from observing the varied features of the spectacle.

A few things I do remember. I remember that the Rotundo, as its name imports, was a circular hall, of large extent, with a flagged floor, an arched ceiling, and white walls.

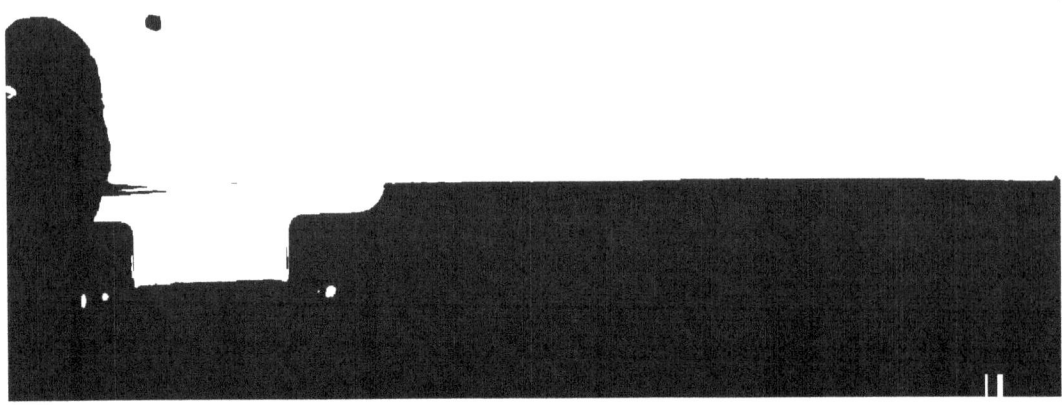

These were without windows, for the hall was lighted from above. On one side, near the wall, stood a desk or rostrum upon an elevated daïs, and by the side of this a large block of cut stone of the form of a parallelopipedon. The use of these two objects I divined.

A stone "kerb," or banquette, ran around one portion of the wall. The purpose of this was equally apparent.

The hall when I entered was half filled with people. They appeared to be of all ages and sorts. They stood conversing in groups, just as men do when assembled for any business, ceremony, or amusement, and waiting for the affair to begin. It was plain, however, from the demeanour of these people, that what they waited for did not impress them with any feelings of solemnity. On the contrary, a merry-meeting might have been anticipated, judging from the rough jests and coarse peals of laughter that from time to time rang through the hall.

There was one group, however, which gave out no such signs or sounds. Seated along the stone banquette, and standing beside it, squatted down upon the floor, or leaning against the wall in any and every attitude, were the individuals of this group. Their black and brown skins, the woolly covering of their skulls, their rough red "brogans," their coarse garments of cheap cottonade, of jeans, of "nigger cloth" died cinnamon colour by the juice of the catalpa-tree,—these characteristics marked them as distinct from all the other groups in the hall—a distinct race of beings.

But even without the distinctions of dress or complexion—even without the thick lips or high cheek-bones and woolly hair, it was easy to tell that those who sat upon the banquette were under different circumstances from these who strutted over the floor. While these talked loudly and laughed gaily, those were silent and sad. These moved about with the air of the conqueror—

those were motionless with the passive look and downcast mien of the captive. These were *masters*—those were *slaves!* They were the slaves of the plantation Besançon.

All were silent, or spoke only in whispers. Most of them seemed ill at ease. Mothers sat holding their " piccaninnies " in their sable embrace, murmuring expressions of endearment, or endeavouring to hush them to rest. Here and there big tears rolled over their swarthy cheeks, as the maternal heart rose and fell with swelling emotions. Fathers looked on with drier eyes, but with the stern helpless gaze of despair, which bespoke the consciousness, that they had no power to avert their fate—no power to undo whatever might be decreed by the pitiless wretches around them.

Not all of them wore this expression. Several of the younger slaves, both boys and girls, were gaily dressed in stuffs of brilliant colours, with flounces, frills, and ribbons. Most of these appeared indifferent to their future. Some even seemed happy—laughing and chatting gaily to each other, or occasionally changing a light word with one of the "white folks." A change of masters could not be such a terrible idea, after the usage they had lately had. Some of them rather anticipated such an event with hopeful pleasure. These were the dandy young men, and the yellow belles of the plantation. They would, perhaps be allowed to remain in that great city, of which they had so often heard—perhaps a brighter future was before them. Dark must it be to be darker than their proximate past.

I glanced over the different groups, but my eyes rested not long upon them. A glance was enough to satisfy me that *she* was not there. There was no danger of mistaking any one of those forms or faces for that of Aurore. She was not there. Thank Heaven!

I was spared the humiliation of seeing her in such a crowd! She was, no doubt, near at hand, and would be brought in when her turn came.

I could ill brook the thought of seeing her exposed to the rude and insulting glances — perhaps insulting speeches — of which she might be the object. And yet that ordeal was in store for me.

I did not discover myself to the slaves. I knew their impulsive natures, and that a scene would be the result. I should be the recipient of their salutations and entreaties, uttered loud enough to draw the attention of all upon me.

To avoid this, I took my station behind one of the groups of white men that screened me from their notice, and kept my eyes fixed upon the entrance, watching for D'Hauteville. In him now lay my last and only hope.

I could not help noting the individuals who passed out and in. Of course they were all of my own sex, but of every variety. There was the regular "negro-trader," a tall lathy fellow, with harsh horse-dealer features, careless dress, loose coat, slouching broad-brimmed hat, coarse boots, and painted quirt of raw hide,—the "cowskin,"—fit emblem of his calling.

In strong contrast to him was the elegantly-attired Creole, in coat of claret or blue, full dress, with gold buttons, plated pantaloons, gaiter "bootees," laced shirt, and diamond studs.

An older variety of the same might be seen in trousers of buff, nankeen jacket of the same material, and hat of Manilla or Panama set over his short-cropped snow-white hair.

The American merchant from Poydras or Tchoupitoulas Street, from Camp, New Levee, or St. Charles, in dress-coat of black cloth, vest of black satin shining like glaze—trousers of like material with the coat—boots of calf-skin, and gloveless hands.

The dandy clerk of steam-boat or store, in white grass frock, snowy ducks, and beaver hat, long furred and of light yellowish hue. There, too, the snug smooth banker—the consequential attorney, here no longer sombre and professional, but gaily caparisoned—the captain of the river-boat, with no naval look—the rich planter of the coast—the proprietor of the cotton press or "pickery"—with a sprinkling of nondescripts made up the crowd that had now assembled in the Rotundo.

As I stood noting these various forms and costumes, a large heavy-built man, with florid face, and dressed in a green "shad-bellied" coat, passed through the entrance. In one hand he carried a bundle of papers, and in the other a small mallet with ivory head—that at once proclaimed his calling.

His entrance produced a buzz, and set the various groups in motion. I could hear the phrases, "Here he comes!" "Yon's him!" "Here comes the major!"

This was not needed to proclaim to all present, who was the individual in the green "shadbelly." The beautiful dome of St. Charles itself was not better known to the citizens of New Orleans than was Major B——, the celebrated auctioneer.

In another minute, the bright bland face of the major appeared above the rostrum. A few smart raps of his hammer commanded silence, and the sale began.

*　　*　　*　　*　　*

Scipio was ordered first upon the block. The crowd of intended bidders pressed around him, poked their fingers between his ribs, felt his limbs as if he had been a fat ox, opened his mouth and examined his teeth as if he had been a horse, and then bid for him just like he had been one or the other.

Under other circumstances I could have felt compassion for the poor fellow; but my heart was too full—there was no room in it for Scipio; and I averted my face from the disgusting spectacle.

CHAPTER IV.

THE SLAVE-MART.

I once more fixed my eyes upon the entrance, scrutinising every form that passed in. As yet no appearance of D'Hauteville! Surely he would soon arrive. He said at twelve o'clock. It was now one, and still he had not come.

No doubt he would come, and in proper time. After all, I need not be so anxious as to the time. Her name was last upon the list. It would be a long time.

I had full reliance upon my new friend —almost unknown, but not untried. His conduct on the previous night had inspired me with perfect confidence. He would not disappoint me. His being thus late did not shake my faith in him. There was some difficulty about his obtaining the money, for it was *money* I expected him to bring. He had hinted as much. No doubt it was that that was detaining him; but he would be in time. He knew that her name was at the bottom of the list — the last *lot* — Lot 65!

Notwithstanding my confidence in D'Hauteville I was ill-at-ease. It was very natural I should be so, and requires no explanation. I kept my gaze upon the door, hoping every moment to see him enter.

Behind me I heard the voice of the auctioneer, in constant and monotonous repetition, interrupted at intervals by the smart rap of his ivory mallet. I knew that the sale was going on! and, by the frequent strokes of the hammer, I could tell that it was rapidly progressing. Although but some half-dozen of the slaves had yet been disposed of, I could not help fancying that they were galloping down the list, and that *her* turn would soon come—too soon. With the fancy my heart beat quicker and wilder. Surely D'Hauteville will not disappoint me?

A group stood near me, talking gaily. They were all young men, and fashionably dressed,—the scions I could tell of the Creole noblesse. They conversed in a tone sufficiently loud for me to overhear them. Perhaps I should not have listened to what they were saying, had not one of them mentioned a particular name that fell harshly upon my ear. The name was *Marigny*. I had an unpleasant recollection associated with this name. It was a Marigny of whom Scipio had spoken to me — a Marigny who had proposed to *purchase Aurore*. Of course I remembered the name.

"Marigny!" I listened.

"So, Marigny, you really intend to bid for her?" asked one.

"*Oui*," replied a young sprig, stylishly and somewhat foppishly dressed. "*Oui— oui — oui*," he continued with a languid drawl, as he drew tighter his lavender gloves, and twirled his tiny cane. "I do intend—*ma foi!*—yes."

"How high will you go?"

"Oh—ah! *une petite somme, mon cher ami.*"

"A *little sum* will not do, Marigny," said the first speaker. "I know half-a-dozen myself who intend bidding for her—rich dogs all of them."

"Who?" inquired Marigny, suddenly awaking from his languid indifference, "Who, may I inquire?"

"Who? Well there's Gardette the dentist, who's half crazed about her; there's the old Marquis; there's planter Villareau and Lebon, of Lafourche; and young Moreau, the wine-merchant of the Rue Dauphin; and who knows but half-a-dozen of those rich Yankee cotton-growers may want her for a *housekeeper!* Ha! ha! ha!

"I can name another," suggested a third speaker.

"Name!" demanded several; "yourself perhaps, Le Ber; you want a sempstress for your shirt-buttons."

"No, not myself," replied the speaker; "I don't buy *coturiers* at that price—*deux mille dollares*, at the least, my friends. *Pardieu!* no. I find my sempstresses at a cheaper rate in the Faubourg Tremé."

"Who, then? Name him!"

"Without hesitation I do,—the old wizen-face Gayarre."

"Gayarre the avocat?"

"M. Dominique Gayarre!"

"Improbable," rejoined one. "M. Gayarre is a man of steady habits—a moralist—a miser!"

"Ha! ha!" laughed Le Ber; "it's plain, Messieurs, you don't understand the character of M. Gayarre. Perhaps I know him better. Miser though he be, in a general sense, there's one class with whom he's generous enough. *Il a une douzaine des maîtresses!* Besides, you must remember that M. Dominique is a bachelor. He wants a good housekeeper—a *femme-de-chambre*. Come, friends, I have heard something—*un petite chose*. I'll lay a wager the miser outbids every one of you,—even rich generous Marigny here!"

Marigny stood biting his lips. His was but a feeling of annoyance or chagrin—mine was utter agony. I had no longer a doubt as to who was the subject of the conversation.

"It was at the suit of Gayarre the bankruptcy was declared, was it not?" asked one.

"'Tis so said."

"Why, he was considered the great friend of the family—the associate of old Besançon?"

"Yes, the *lawyer-friend* of the family—Ha! ha!" significantly rejoined another.

"Poor Eugénie! she'll be no longer the belle. She'll now be less difficult to please in her choice of a husband."

"That's some consolation for you, Le Ber. Ha! ha!"

"Oh!" interposed another, "Le Ber had no chance lately. There's a young Englishman the favourite now—the same who swam ashore with her at the blowing-up of the Belle steamer. So I have heard, at least. Is it so, Le Ber?"

"You had better inquire of Mademoiselle Besançon," replied the latter, in a peevish tone, at which the others laughed.

"I would," replied the questioner, "but I know not where to find her. Where is she? She's not at her plantation. I was up there, and she had left two days before. She's not with the aunt here. Where is she, Monsieur?"

I listened for the answer to this question with a degree of interest. I, too, was ignorant of the whereabouts of Eugénie, and had sought for her that day, but in vain. It was said she had come to the city, but no one could tell me anything of her. And

I now remembered what she had said in her letter of "*Sacré Cœur.*" Perhaps, thought I, she has really gone to the convent. Poor Eugénie!

"Aye, where is she, Monsieur?" asked another of the party.

"Very strange!" said several at once. "Where can she be? Le Ber, you must know."

"I know nothing of the movements of Mademoiselle Besançon," answered the young man, with an air of chagrin and surprise, too, as if he was really ignorant upon the subject, as well as vexed by the remarks which his companions were making.

"There's something mysterious in all this," continued one of the number. "I should be astonished at it, if it were any one else than Eugénie Besançon."

It is needless to say that this conversation interested *me*. Every word of it fell like a spark of fire upon my heart; and I could have strangled these fellows, one and all of them, as they stood. Little knew they that the "young Englishman" was near, listening to them, and as little the dire effect their words were producing.

It was not what they said of Eugénie that gave me pain. It was their free speech about Aurore. I have not repeated their ribald talk in relation to her—their jesting inuendoes, their base hypotheses, and coldly-brutal sneers whenever her chastity was named.

One in particular, a certain M. Sévigné, was more *bizarre* than any of his companions; and once or twice I was upon the point of turning upon him. It cost me an effort to restrain myself, but that effort was successful, and I stood unmoved. Perhaps I should not have been able to endure it much longer, but for the interposition of an event, which at once drove these gossips and their idle talk out of my mind. That event was *the entrance of Aurore!*

They had again commenced speaking of

her—of her chastity—of her rare charms. They were discussing the probabilities as to who would become possessed of her, and the *certainty* that she would be the *maîtresse* of whoever did; they were waxing warmer in their eulogium of her beauty, and beginning to lay wagers on the result of the sale, when all at once the clack of their conversation ceased, and two or three cried out,—

"*Voilà! voilà! elle vient!*"

I turned mechanically at the words. Aurore was in the entrance!

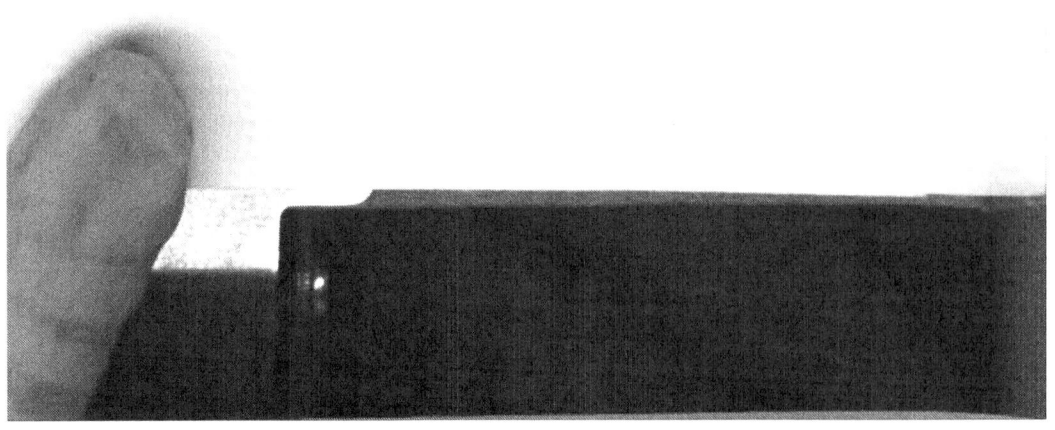

CHAPTER V.

BIDDING FOR MY BETROTHED.

Yes, Aurore appeared in the doorway of that infernal hall, and stood timidly pausing upon its threshold.

She was not alone. A mulatto girl was by her side—like herself a slave—like herself, brought there *to be sold!*

A third individual was of the party, or rather with it; for he did not walk by the side of the girls, but in front, evidently conducting them to the place of sale. This individual was no other than Larkin, the brutal overseer.

"Come along!" said he roughly, at the same time beckoning to Aurore and her companion: "this way, gals—foller me!"

They obeyed his rude signal, and, passing in, followed him across the hall towards the rostrum.

I stood with slouched hat and averted face. Aurore saw me not.

As soon as they were fairly past, and their backs towards me, my eyes followed them. Oh! beautiful Aurore!—beautiful as ever!

I was not single in my admiration. The appearance of the quadroon created a sensation. The din ceased as if by a signal; every voice became hushed, and every eye was bent upon her as she moved across the floor. Men hurried forward from distant parts of the hall to get a nearer glance; others made way for her, stepping politely back as if she had been a queen. Men did this, who would have scorned to offer politeness to another of her race—to the "yellow girl," for instance, who walked by her side!

Oh, the power of beauty! Never was it more markedly shown than in the *entrée* of that poor slave.

I heard the whispers, I observed the glances of admiration, of passion. I marked the longing eyes that followed her, noting her splendid form and its undulating outlines as she moved forward.

All this gave me pain. It was a feeling worse than mere jealousy I experienced. It was jealousy embittered by the very brutality of my rivals.

Aurore was simply attired. There was no affectation of the fine lady—none of the ribbons and flounces that bedecked the dress of her darker-skinned companion. Such would have ill assorted with the noble melancholy that appeared upon her beautiful countenance. None of all this.

A robe of light-coloured muslin, tastefully made, with long skirt and tight sleeves —as was the fashion of the time—a fashion that displayed the pleasing rotundity of her figure. Her head-dress was that worn by all quadroons,—the "toque" of the Madras kerchief, which sat upon her brow like a coronet, its green, crimson, and yellow checks contrasting finely with the raven blackness of her hair. She wore no ornaments excepting the broad gold rings that glittered against the rich glow of her cheeks; and upon her finger one other circlet of gold—the token of her betrothal. I knew it well.

I buried myself in the crowd, slouching my hat on that side towards the rostrum. I desired she should not see me, while I could not help gazing upon *her*. I had taken my stand in such a situation, that I could still command a view of the entrance. More than ever was I anxious about the coming of D'Hauteville.

Aurore had been placed near the foot of the rostrum. I could just see the edge of her turban over the shoulders of the crowd. By elevating myself on my toes, I could observe her face, which by chance was turned towards me. Oh! how my heart heaved as I struggled to read its expression—as I endeavoured to divine the subject of her thoughts!

She looked sad and anxious. That was natural enough. But I looked for another expression—that unquiet anxiety produced by the alternation of hope and fear.

Her eye wandered over the crowd. She scanned the sea of faces that surrounded her. *She was searching for some one. Was it for me?*

I held down my face as her glance passed over the spot. I dared not meet her gaze. I feared that I could not restrain myself from addressing her. Sweet Aurore!

I again looked up. Her eye was still wandering in fruitless search — oh! surely it is for me!

Again I cowered behind the crowd, and her glance was carried onward.

I raised myself once more. I saw the

shadow darkening upon her face. Her eye filled with a deeper expression — it was the look of despair!

"Courage! courage!" I whispered to myself. "Look again, lovely Aurore! This time I shall meet you. I shall speak to you from mine eyes — I shall give back glance for glance ——

"She sees — she recognises me! That start — the flash of joy in her eyes — the smile curling upon her lips! Her glance wanders no more—her gaze is fixed—proud heart! It *was* for me!"

Yes, our eyes met at length — met melting and swimming with love. Mine had escaped from my control. For some moments I could not turn them aside, but surrendered them to the impulse of my passion. It was mutual. I doubted it not. I felt as though the ray of love-light was passing between us. I had almost forgotten where I stood!

A murmur from the crowd, and a movement, restored me to my senses. Her steadfast gaze had been noticed, and by many—skilled to interpret such glances—had been understood. These, in turning round to see who was the object of that glance, had caused the movement. I had observed it in time, and turned my face in another direction.

I watched the entrance for D'Hauteville. Why had he not arrived? My anxiety increased with the minutes.

True, it would still be an hour—perhaps two—before *her* time should come.—— Ha!—what?

There was silence for a moment—something of interest was going on. I looked toward the rostrum for an explanation. A dark man had climbed upon one of the steps, and was whispering to the auctioneer.

He remained but a moment. He appeared to have asked some favour, which was at once conceded him, and he stepped back to his place among the crowd.

A minute or two intervened, and then, to my horror and astonishment, I saw the overseer take Aurore by the arm, and raise her upon the block! The intention was plain. *She was to be sold next!*

In the moments that followed, I cannot remember exactly how I acted. I ran wildly for the entrance. I looked out into the street. Up and down I glanced with anxious eyes. No D'Hauteville!

I rushed back into the hall, — again through the outer circles of the crowd, in the direction of the rostrum.

The bidding had begun. I had not heard the preliminaries, but as I re-entered there fell upon my ear the terrible words; —

"*A thousand dollars for the quadroon! — A thousand dollars bid!*"

"O Heaven! D'Hauteville has deceived me. She is lost! — lost!"

In my desperation I was about to interrupt the sale. I was about to proclaim aloud its unfairness, in the fact that the

quadroon had been *taken out of the order advertised!* Even on this poor plea I rested a hope.

It was the straw to the drowning man, but I was determined to grasp it.

I had opened my lips to call out, when some one pulling me by the sleeve caused me to turn round. It was D'Hauteville! Thank Heaven, it was D'Hauteville!

I could scarce restrain myself from shouting with joy. His look told me that he was the bearer of bright gold.

"In time, and none to spare," whispered he, thrusting a pocket-book between my fingers; "there is three thousand dollars — that will surely be enough; 'tis all I have been able to procure. I cannot stay here — there are those I do not wish to see. I shall meet you after the sale is over. Adieu!"

I scarce thanked him. I saw not his parting. My eyes were elsewhere.

"Fifteen hundred dollars bid for the

quadroon!—good housekeeper—sempstress—fifteen hundred dollars!"

"*Two thousand!*" I called out, my voice husky with emotion.

The sudden leap over such a large sum drew the attention of the crowd upon me. Looks, smiles, and inuendoes, were freely exchanged at my expense.

I saw, or rather heeded them not. I saw Aurore—only Aurore—standing upon the daïs like a statue upon its pedestal—the type of sadness and beauty. The sooner I could take her thence, the happier for me; and with that object in view I had made my "bid."

"Two thousand dollars bid — two thousand — twenty-one hundred dollars — two thousand, one, two — twenty-two hundred dollars bid—twenty-two ——"

"Twenty-five hundred dollars!" I again cried out, in as firm a voice as I could command.

"Twenty-five hundred dollars," repeated

the auctioneer, in his monotonous drawl; "*twenty-five — six —* you, sir? thank you! twenty-six hundred dollars for the quadroon —twenty-six hundred!"

"Oh God! they will go above three thousand—if they do ——"

"Twenty-seven hundred dollars!" bid the fop Marigny.

"Twenty-eight hundred!" from the old Marquis.

"Twenty-eight hundred and fifty!" assented the young merchant, Moreau.

"Nine!" nodded the tall dark man who had whispered to the auctioneer.

"Twenty-nine hundred dollars bid—two thousand nine hundred."

"Three thousand!" I gasped out in despair.

It was my last bid. I could go no farther.

I waited for the result — as the condemned waits for the falling of the trap or the descent of the axe. My heart could not have endured very long that terrible suspense. But I had not long to endure it.

"*Three thousand one hundred dollars!*——three thousand one hundred bid—thirty-one hundred dollars ——"

I cast one look upon Aurore. It was a look of hopeless despair; and, turning away, I staggered mechanically across the hall.

Before I had reached the entrance I could hear the voice of the auctioneer, in the same prolonged drawl, calling out, — "Three thousand five hundred bid for the quadroon girl!"

I halted and listened. The sale was coming to its close.

"Three thousand five hundred—going at three thousand five hundred — going — going ——"

The sharp stroke of the hammer fell upon my ear. It drowned the final word "gone!" but my heart pronounced that word in the emphasis of its agony.

There was a noisy scene of confusion—

loud words and high excitement among the crowd of disappointed bidders. Who was the fortunate one?

I leant over to ascertain. The tall dark man was in conversation with the auctioneer. Aurore stood beside him. I now remembered having seen the man on the boat. He was the agent of whom D'Hauteville had spoken. The Creole had guessed aright, and so, too, had Le Ber.

Gayarre had outbid them all!

CHAPTER VI.

THE HACKNEY-CARRIAGE.

For a while I lingered in the hall, irresolute and almost without purpose. She whom I loved, and who loved me in return, was wrested from me by an infamous law—ruthlessly torn from me. She would be borne away before my eyes, and I might, perhaps, never behold her again. Probable enough was this thought,—I might never behold her again! Lost to me, more hopelessly lost, than if she had become the *bride* of another. Far more hopelessly lost. Then, at least, she would have been free to think, to act, to go abroad, to ——. Then, I might have hoped to meet her again — to see her — to gaze upon her, even if only at a distance—to worship her in the secret silence of my heart — to console myself with the belief that she still loved me. Yes; the bride, the wife of another! Even that I could have borne with calmness. But now, not the bride of another, but the *slave*—the forced unwilling *leman* — and that other ———. Oh! how my heart writhed under its horrible imaginings!

What next? How was I to act? Resign myself to the situation? Make no further effort to recover—to save her?

No! It had not come to that. Discouraging as the prospect was, a ray of hope was visible; one ray yet illumed the dark future, sustaining and bracing my mind for further action.

The plan was still undefined; but the purpose had been formed—and that purpose was to free Aurore—to make her mine *at every hazard!* I thought no longer of buying her. I knew that Gayarre had become her owner. I felt satisfied that to purchase her was no longer possible. He who had paid such an enormous sum would not be likely to part with her at any price. My whole fortune would not suffice. I gave not a thought to it. I felt certain it would be impossible.

Far different was the resolve that was already forming itself in my mind, and cheering me with new hopes. Forming itself, do I say? It had already taken a definite shape—even before the echoes of the salesman's voice had died upon my ears! With the clink of his hammer my mind was made up. The purpose was formed; it was only the *plan* that remained indefinite.

I had resolved to outrage the laws—to become thief or robber, whichever it might please circumstances to make me. I had resolved to *steal my betrothed!*

Disgrace there might be—danger I knew there was, not only to my liberty, but my life. I cared but little about the disgrace; I recked not of the danger. My purpose was fixed—my determination taken.

Brief had been the mental process that conducted me to this determination—the more brief that the thought had passed through my mind before—the more brief that I believed there was positively no other means I could adopt. It was the only course of action left me—either that, or yield up all that I loved without a struggle—and, passion-led as I was, I was not going to yield. Certain disgrace,—even death itself, appeared more welcome than this alternative.

I had formed not yet the shadow of a plan. That must be thought of afterward, but even at that moment was action required. My poor heart was on the rack; I could not bear the thought that a single night should pass, and she under the same roof with that hideous man!

Wherever she should pass the night, I was determined that I should not be far distant from her. Walls might separate us, but she should know I was near. Just that much of a plan *had* I thought of.

Stepping to a retired spot, I took out my note-book, and wrote upon one of its leaves:

" *Ce soir viendrai!*—Edouard."

I had no time to be more particular, for I feared every moment she would be hurried out of my sight. I tore out the leaf; and, hastily folding it, returned to the entrance of the Rotundo.

Just as I got back to the door a hackney carriage drove up, and halted in front. I conjectured its use, and lost no time in providing another from a stand close by. This done, I returned within the hall. I was yet in time. As I entered, I saw Aurore being led away from the rostrum.

I pressed into the crowd, and stood in such a position that she would have to pass near me. As she did so, our hands met, and the note parted from my fingers. There was no time for a further recognition — not even a love-pressure—for the moment after she was hurried on through the crowd, and the carriage-door closed after her.

The mulatto girl accompanied her, and another of the female slaves. All were put into the carriage. The negro-dealer climbed to the box alongside the coachman, and the vehicle rattled off over the stony pavement.

A word to my driver was enough, who, giving the whip to his horses, followed at like speed.

CHAPTER VII.

TO BRINGIERS.

Coachmen of New Orleans possess their full share of *intelligence*, and the ring of a piece of silver, extra of their fare, is a music well understood by them. They are the witnesses of many a romantic adventure—the necessary confidants of many a love-secret. A hundred yards in front rolled the carriage that had taken Aurore;—now turning round corners, now passing among drays laden with huge cotton bales or hogsheads of sugar—but my driver had fixed his knowing eye upon it, and I had no need to be uneasy.

It passed up the Rue Chartres but a short distance, and then turned into one of the short streets that ran from this at right angles towards the Levee. I fancied for a moment, it was making for the steamboat wharves; but on reaching the corner, I saw that it had stopped about half-way down the street. My driver, according to the instructions I had given him, pulled up at the corner, and awaited my further orders.

The carriage I had followed was now standing in front of a house; and just as I rounded the corner, I caught a glimpse of several figures crossing the banquette and entering the door. No doubt, all that had ridden in the carriage—Aurore with the rest—had gone inside the house.

Presently a man came out, and handing his fare to the hackney-coachman, turned and went back into the house. The latter, gathering up his reins, gave the whip to his horses, and, wheeling round, came back by the Rue Chartres. As he passed me, I glanced through the open windows of his vehicle. It was empty. She had gone into the house, then.

I had no longer any doubt as to where she had been taken. I read on the corner, "Rue Bienville." The house where the carriage had stopped was the town residence of M. Dominique Gayarre.

I remained for some minutes in the cab, considering what I had best do. Was this to be her future home? or was she only brought here temporarily, to be afterwards taken up to the plantation?

Some thought, or instinct perhaps, whispered me that she was not to remain in the Rue Bienville; but would be carried to the gloomy old mansion at Bringiers. I cannot tell why I thought so. Perhaps it was, because I wished it so.

I saw the necessity of watching the house —so that she might not be taken away without my knowing it. Wherever she went I was determined to follow.

Fortunately I was prepared for any journey. The three thousand dollars lent me by D'Hauteville remained intact. With that I could travel to the ends of the earth.

I wished that the young Creole had been with me. I wanted his counsel—his company. How should I find him? He had not said where we should meet—only that he would join me when the sale should be over. I saw nothing of him on leaving the Rotundo. Perhaps he meant to meet me there or at my hotel; but how was I to get back to either of these places without leaving my post?

I was perplexed as to how I should communicate with D'Hauteville. It occurred to me that the hackney-coachman—I had not yet dismissed him—might remain and watch the house, while I went in search of the Creole. I had only to pay the Jehu; he would obey me, of course, and right willingly.

I was about arranging with the man, and had already given him some instructions, when I heard wheels rumbling along the street; and a somewhat old-fashioned coach, drawn by a pair of mules, turned into the Rue Bienville. A negro driver was upon the box.

There was nothing odd in all this. Such a carriage and such a coachman were to be seen every hour in New Orleans, and drawn by mules as often as horses. But this pair of mules, and the negro who drove them, I recognised.

Yes! I recognised the equipage. I had often met it upon the Levee Road near Bringiers. It was the carriage of M. Dominique!

I was further assured upon this point by seeing the vehicle draw up in front of the avocat's house.

I at once gave up my design of going back for D'Hauteville. Climbing back into the hack, I ensconced myself in such a position, that I could command a view of what passed in the Rue Bienville.

Some one was evidently about to become the occupant of the carriage. The door of the house stood open, and a servant was speaking to the coachman. I could tell by the actions of the latter, that he expected soon to drive off.

The servant now appeared outside with several parcels, which he placed upon the coach; then a man came out—the negro-trader—who mounted the box. Another man shot across the banquette, but in such a hurried gait that I could not recognise him. I guessed, however, who *he* was. Two others now came from the house — a mulatto woman and a young girl. In spite of the cloak in which she was enveloped, I recognised Aurore. The mulatto woman conducted the girl to the carriage, and then stepped in after. At this moment a man on horseback appeared in the street, and riding up, halted by the carriage. After speaking to some one inside, he again put his horse in motion and rode off. This horseman was Larkin the overseer.

The clash of the closing door was immediately followed by the crack of the coachman's whip; and the mules, trotting off down the street, turned to the right, and headed up the Levee.

My driver, who had already been instructed, gave the whip to his hack, and followed keeping a short distance in the rear.

It was not till we had traversed the long street of Tchoupitoulas, through the Faubourg Marigny, and were some distance upon the road to the suburban village of Lafayette, that I thought of where I was going. My sole idea had been to keep in sight the carriage of Gayarre.

I now bethought me for what purpose I was driving after him. Did I intend to follow him to his house, some thirty miles distant, in a hackney-coach?

Even had I been so determined, it was questionable whether the driver of the vehicle could have been tempted to humour my caprice, or whether his wretched hack could have accomplished such a feat.

For what purpose, then, was I galloping after? To overtake these men upon the road, and deliver Aurore from their keeping? No, there were three of them—well armed, no doubt—and I alone!

But it was not until I had gone several miles that I began to reflect on the absurdity of my conduct. I then ordered my coachman to pull up.

I remained seated; and from the window of the hack gazed after the carriage, until it was hidden by a turn in the road.

"After all," I muttered to myself, "I have done right in following. I am now sure of their destination. Back to the Hotel St. Luis!"

The last phrase was a command to my

coachman, who turning his horse drove back.

As I had promised to pay for speed, it was not long before the wheels of my hackney rattled over the pave of the Rue St. Luis.

Having dismissed the carriage, I entered the hotel. To my joy I found D'Hauteville awaiting my return; and in a few minutes I had communicated to him my determination to carry off Aurore.

Rare friendship his! he approved of my resolve. Rare devotion! he proposed to take part in my enterprise!

I warned him of its perils—to no purpose. With an enthusiasm I could not account for, and that greatly astonished me at the time, he still insisted upon sharing them.

Perhaps I might more earnestly have admonished him against such a purpose, but I felt how much I stood in need of him.

I could not explain the strange feeling of confidence, with which the presence of this gentle but heroic youth had inspired me. The reluctance with which I accepted his offer was only apparent—it was not felt. My heart was struggling against my will. I was but too glad when he stated his determination to accompany me.

There was no boat going up that night; but we were not without the means to travel. A pair of horses were hired—the best that money could procure—and before sun-down we had cleared the suburbs of the city, and were riding along the road that conducts to the village of Bringiers.

CHAPTER VIII.

TWO VILLAINS.

WE travelled rapidly. There were no hills to impede our progress. Our route lay along the Levee Road, which leads from New Orleans by the bank of the river, passing plantations and settlements at every few hundred yards' distance. The path was as level as a race-course, and the hoof fell gently upon the soft dusty surface, enabling us to ride with ease. The horses we bestrode were *mustangs* from the prairies of Texas, trained to that gait, the "pace" peculiar to the saddle-nags of the South-western States. Excellent "pacers" both were; and, before the night came down, we had made more than half of our journey.

Up to this time we had exchanged only a few words. I was busy with my thoughts—busy planning my enterprise. My young companion appeared equally occupied with his.

The darkening down of the night brought us closer together; and I now unfolded to D'Hauteville the plan which I had proposed to myself.

There was not much of plan about it. My intention was simply thus: To proceed at once to the plantation of Gayarre—stealthily to approach the house—to communicate with Aurore through some of the slaves of the plantation; failing in this, to find out, if possible, in what part of the house she would pass the night—to enter her room after all had gone to sleep—propose to her to fly with me—and then make our escape the best way we could.

Once clear of the house, I had scarce thought of a plan of action. That seemed easy enough. Our horses would carry us back to the city. There we might remain concealed, until some friendly ship should bear us from the country.

This was all the plan I had conceived, and having communicated it to D'Hauteville, I awaited his response.

After some moments' silence, he replied, signifying his approval of it. Like me, he could think of no other course to be followed. Aurore must be carried away at all hazards.

We now conversed about the details. We debated every chance of failure and success.

Our main difficulty, both agreed, would be in communicating with Aurore. Could we do so? Surely she would not be locked in? Surely Gayarre would not be suspicious enough to have her guarded and watched? He was now the full owner of this coveted treasure—no one could legally deprive him of his slave—no one could carry her away without the risk of a fearful punishment;

and although he no doubt suspected that some understanding existed between the quadroon and myself, he would never dream of such a love as that which I felt—a love that would lead me to risk even life itself, as I now intended.

No. Gayarre, judging from his own vile passion, might believe that I, like himself, had been " struck " with the girl's beauty, and that I was willing to pay a certain sum —three thousand dollars—to possess her. But the fact that I had bid no more—no doubt exactly reported to him by his agent —was proof that my love had its limits, and there was an end of it. As a rival he would hear of me no more. No. M. Dominique Gayarre would never suspect a passion like mine—would never dream of such a purpose as the one to which that passion now impelled me. An enterprise so romantic was not within the bounds of probability. Therefore—so reasoned D'Hauteville and I—it was not likely Aurore would be either guarded or watched.

But even though she might not be, how were we to communicate with her? That would be extremely difficult.

I built my hopes on the little slip of paper—on the words "*Ce soir viendrai.*" Surely upon this night Aurore would *not sleep*. My heart told me she would not, and the thought rendered me proud and sanguine. That very night should I make the attempt to carry her off. I could not bear the thought that she should pass even a single night under the roof of her tyrant.

And the night promised to befriend us. The sun had scarcely gone down, when the sky became sullen, turning to the hue of lead. As soon as the short twilight passed, the whole canopy had grown so dark, that we could scarce distinguish the outline of the forest from the sky itself. Not a star could be seen. A thick pall of smoke-coloured clouds hid them from the view. Even the yellow surface of the river was scarce perceptible from its bank, and the white dust of the road alone guided us.

In the woods, or upon the darker ground of the plantation fields, to find a path would have been impossible—so intense was the darkness that enveloped us.

We might have augured trouble from this —we might have feared losing our way. But I was not afraid of any such result. I felt assured that the star of love itself would guide me.

The darkness would be in our favour. Under its friendly shadow we could approach the house, and act with safety; whereas had it been a moonlight night, we should have been in great danger of being discovered.

I read in the sudden change of sky no ill augury, but an omen of success.

There were signs of an approaching storm. What to me would have been kindly weather? Anything—a rain-storm—a tempest

—a hurricane—anything but a fine night was what I desired.

It was still early when we reached the plantation Besançon—not quite midnight. We had lost no time on the road. Our object in hurrying forward was to arrive at the place before the household of Gayarre should go to rest. Our hopes were that we might find some means of communicating with Aurore—through the slaves.

One of these I knew. I had done him a slight favour during my residence at Bringiers. I had gained his confidence—enough to render him accessible to a bribe. He might be found, and might render us the desired assistance.

All was silent upon the plantation Besançon. The dwelling-house appeared deserted. There were no lights to be seen. One glimmered in the rear, in a window of the overseer's house. The negro quarter was dark and silent. The buzz usual at that hour was not heard. They whose voices used to echo through its little street, were now far away. The cabins were empty. The song, the jest, and the cheerful laugh, were hushed; and the 'coon-dog, howling for his absent master, was the only sound that broke the stillness of the place.

We passed the gate, riding in silence, and watching the road in front of us. We were observing the greatest caution as we advanced. We might meet those whom above all others we desired not to encounter —the overseer, the agent, Gayarre himself. Even to have been seen by one of Gayarre's negroes might have resulted in the defeat of our plans. So fearful was I of this, that but for the darkness of the night, I should have left the road sooner, and tried a path through the woods which I knew of. It was too dark to traverse this path without difficulty and loss of time. We therefore clung to the road, intending to leave it when we should arrive opposite the plantation of Gayarre.

Between the two plantations a wagon-road for wood-hauling led to the forest. It was this road I intended to take. We should not be likely to meet any one upon it; and it was our design to conceal our horses' among the trees in the rear of the cane-fields. On such a night not even the negro 'coon-hunter would have any business in the woods.

Creeping along with caution, we had arrived near the point where this wood-road *debouched*, when voices reached our ears. Some persons were coming down the road.

We reined up and listened. There were men in conversation; and from their voices each moment growing more distinct, we could tell that they were approaching us.

They were coming down the main road from the direction of the village. The hoof-stroke told us they were on horseback, and, consequently, that they were white men.

A large cotton-wood tree stood on the waste ground on one side of the road. The long flakes of Spanish moss hanging from its branches nearly touched the ground. It offered the readiest place of concealment, and we had just time to spur our horses behind its giant trunk, when the horsemen came abreast of the tree.

Dark as it was, we could see them in passing. Their forms—two of them there were — were faintly outlined against the yellow surface of the water. Had they been silent, we might have remained in ignorance as to who they were, but their voices betrayed them. They were Larkin and the trader.

"Good!" whispered D'Hauteville as we recognised them—"they have left Gayarre's—they are on their way home to the plantation Besançon."

The very same thought had occurred to myself. No doubt they were returning to their homes—the overseer to the plantation Besançon, and the trader to his own house—which I knew to be farther down the coast.

I now remembered having often seen this man in company with Gayarre.

The thought had occurred to myself as D'Hauteville spoke, but how knew *he?* He must be well acquainted with the country, thought I.

I had no time to reflect or ask him any question. The conversation of these two ruffians—for ruffians both were—occupied all my attention. They were evidently in high glee, laughing as they went, and jesting as they talked. No doubt their vile work had been remunerative.

"Wal, Bill," said the trader, "it air the biggest price I ever gin for a nigger."

"Darn the old French fool! He's paid well for his whistle this time—he ain't allers so open-fisted. Dog darned if he is!"

"Wal—she air dear; an she ain't, when a man has the dollars to spare. She's as putty a piece o' goods as there air in all Louisiana. I wouldn't mind myself——"

"Ha! ha! ha!" boisterously laughed the overseer. "I guess you can get a chance if you've a mind to," he added, in a significant way.

"Say, Bill!—tell me—be candid, old feller—have you ever ——?"

"Wal, to tell the truth I hain't,—but I reckon I mout if I had pushed the thing. I wan't long enough on the plantation. Beside, she's so stuck up with cussed pride an larnin', that she thinks herself as good as white. I calclate old Foxey 'll bring down her notions a bit. She won't be long wi' him till she'll be glad to take a ramble in the woods wi' anybody that asks her. There 'll be chance enough yet, I reckon."

The trader muttered some reply to this prophetic speech; but both were now so distant that their conversation was no longer audible. What I had heard, absurd as it was, caused me a feeling of pain, and, if possible, heightened my desire to save Aurore from the terrible fate that awaited her.

Giving the word to my companion, we rode out from behind the tree, and a few minutes after turned into the bye-path that led to the woods.

CHAPTER IX.

THE PAWPAW THICKET.

Our progress along this bye-road was slow. There was no white dust upon the path to guide us. We had to grope our way as well as we could between the zigzag fences. Now and then our horses stumbled in the deep ruts made by the wood-wagons, and it was with difficulty we could force them forward.

My companion seemed to manage better than I, and whipped his horse onward as if he were more familiar with the path or else more reckless! I wondered at this without making any remark.

After half-an-hour's struggling, we reached the angle of the rail-fence, where the enclosure ended and the woods began. Another hundred yards brought us under the shadow of the tall timber; where we reined up to take breath, and concert what was next to be done.

I remembered that there was a pawpaw thicket near this place.

"If we could find it," I said to my companion, "and leave our horses there?"

"We may easily do that," was the reply; "though 'tis scarce worth while searching for a thicket—the darkness will sufficiently conceal them.—Ha! not so—*Voilà l'éclair!*"

As D'Hauteville spoke a blue flash lit up the whole canopy of heaven. Even the gloomy aisles of the forest were illuminated, so that we could distinguish the trunks and branches of the trees to a long distance around us. The light wavered for some seconds, like a lamp about being extinguished; and then went suddenly out, leaving the darkness more opaque than before.

There was no noise accompanying this phenomenon—at least none produced by the lightning itself. It caused some noise, however, among the wild creatures of the woods. It woke the white-headed haliaetus perched upon the head of the tall taxodium, and his maniac laugh sounded harsh and shrill. It woke the grallatores of the swamp — the qua-bird, the curlews, and the tall blue herons — who screamed in concert. The owl, already awake, hooted louder its solemn note; and from the deep profound of the forest came the howl of the wolf, and the more thrilling cry of the cougar.

All nature seemed startled by this sudden blaze of light that filled the firmament. But the moment after all was darkness and silence as before.

"The storm will soon be on?" I suggested.

"No," said my companion, "there will be no storm—you hear no thunder—when it is thus we shall have no rain—a very black night, with lightning at intervals,—nothing more. Again!"

The exclamation was drawn forth by a

second blaze of lightning, that like the first lit up the woods on all sides around us, and, as before, unaccompanied by thunder. Neither the slightest rumble nor clap was heard, but the wild creatures once more uttered their varied cries.

"We must conceal the horses then," said my companion; "some straggler might be abroad, and with this light they could be seen far off. The pawpaw thicket is the very place. Let us seek it! It lies in this direction."

D'Hauteville rode forward among the tree-trunks. I followed mechanically. I felt satisfied he knew the ground better than I! He must have been here before, was my reflection.

We had not gone many steps before the blue light blazed a third time; and we could see, directly in front of us, the smooth shining branches and broad green leaves of the *Asiminas*, forming the underwood of the forest.

When the lightning flashed again, we had entered the thicket.

Dismounting in its midst, we hastily tied our bridles to the branches; and then, leaving our horses to themselves, we returned towards the open ground.

Ten minutes' walking enabled us to regain the zigzag railing that shut in the plantation of Gayarre.

Directing ourselves along this, in ten minutes after we arrived opposite the house —which by the electric blaze we could distinguish shining among the tall cotton-wood trees that grew around it. At this point we again made a stop to reconnoitre the ground, and consider how we should proceed.

A wide field stretched from the fence almost to the walls. A garden enclosed by palings lay between the field and the house; and on one side we could perceive the roofs of numerous cabins denoting the negro quarter. At some distance in the same direction, stood the sugar-mill and other outbuildings, and near these the house of Gayarre's overseer.

This point was to be avoided. Even the negro quarter must be shunned, lest we might give alarm. The dogs would be our worst enemies. I knew that Gayarre kept several. I had often seen them along the roads. Large fierce animals they were. How were they to be shunned? They would most likely be rambling about the outbuildings or the negro cabins; therefore, our safest way would be to approach from the opposite side.

If we should fail to discover the apartment of Aurore, then it would be time to make reconnoissance in the direction of the "quarter," and endeavour to find the boy Caton.

We saw lights in the house. Several windows—all upon the ground-floor—were shining through the darkness. More than one apartment therefore was occupied.

This gave us hope. One of them might be occupied by Aurore.

"And now, Monsieur!" said D'Hauteville, after we had discussed the various details, "suppose we fail? suppose some alarm be given, and we be detected before ——?"

I turned, and looking my young companion full in the face, interrupted him in what he was about to say. "D'Hauteville!" said I, "perhaps, I may never be able to repay your generous friendship. It has already exceeded all bounds—but *life* you must not risk for me. That I cannot permit."

"And how risk life, Monsieur?"

"If I fail—if alarm be given—if I am opposed, *voilà*—— !"

I opened the breast of my coat, exposing to his view my pistols.

"Yes!" I continued; "I am reckless enough. I shall use them if necessary. I shall take life if it stand in the way. I am resolved; but you must not risk an encounter. You must remain here—I shall go to the house alone."

"No—no!" he answered promptly; "I go with you."

"I cannot permit it, Monsieur. It is better for you to remain here. You can stay by the fence until I return to you —until *we* return, I should say, for I come not back without *her*."

"Do not act rashly, Monsieur!"

"No, but I am determined. I am desperate. You must not go farther."

"And why not? *I, too, have an interest in this affair.*"

"You?" I asked, surprised at the words as well as the tone in which they were spoken. "You an interest?"

"Of course," coolly replied my companion. "I love adventure. That gives me an interest. You must permit me to accompany you—I must go along with you!"

"As you will then, Monsieur D'Hauteville. Fear not! I shall act with prudence. Come on!"

I sprang over the fence, followed by my companion; and, without another word having passed between us, we struck across the field in the direction of the house.

CHAPTER X.

THE ELOPEMENT.

It was a field of sugar-cane. The canes were of that species known as "ratoons"— suckers from old roots — and the thick bunches at their bases, as well as the tall columns, enabled us to pass among them unobserved. Even had it been day, we might have approached the house unseen.

We soon reached the garden-paling. Here we stopped to reconnoitre the ground. A short survey was sufficient. We saw the very place where we could approach and conceal ourselves.

The house had an antique weather-beaten look — not without some pretensions to grandeur. It was a wooden building, two stories in height, with gable roofs, and large windows — all of which had venetian shutters that opened to the outside. Both walls and window-shutters had once been painted, but the paint was old and rusty; and the colour of the venetians, once green, could hardly be distinguished from the grey wood-work of the walls. All round the house ran an open gallery or verandah, raised some three or four feet from the ground. Upon this gallery the windows and doors opened, and a paling or guard-rail encompassed the whole. Opposite the doors, a stairway of half-a-dozen steps led up; but at all other parts the space underneath was open in front, so that, by stooping a little, one might get under the floor of the gallery.

By crawling close up in front of the verandah, and looking through the rails, we should be able to command a full view of all the windows in the house; and in case of alarm, we could conceal ourselves in the dark cavity underneath. We should be safe there, unless scented by the dogs.

Our plan was matured in whispers. It was not much of a plan. We were to advance to the edge of the verandah, peep through the windows until we could discover the apartment of Aurore; then do our best to communicate with her, and get her out. Our success depended greatly upon accident or good fortune.

Before we could make a move forward, fortune seemed as though she was going to favour us. In one of the windows, directly before our face, a figure appeared. A glance told us it was the quadroon!

The window, as before stated, reached down to the floor of the verandah; and as the figure appeared behind the glass, we could see it from head to foot. The Madras kerchief on the head, the gracefully undulating figure, outlined upon the background of the lighted room, left no doubt upon our minds as to who it was.

" 'Tis Aurore!" whispered my companion.

How could *he* tell? Did he know her? Ah! I remembered—he had seen her that morning in the Rotundo.

"It is she!" I replied, my beating heart scarce allowing me to make utterance.

The window was curtained, but she had raised the curtain in one hand, and was looking out. There was that in her attitude that betokened earnestness. She appeared as if trying to penetrate the gloom. Even in the distance I could perceive this, and my heart bounded with joy. She had understood my note. She was looking for me!

D'Hauteville thought so as well. Our prospects were brightening. If she guessed our design, our task would be easier.

She remained but a few moments by the window. She turned away, and the curtain dropped into its place; but before it had screened the view, the dark shadow of a man fell against the back wall of the room. Gayarre, no doubt!

I could hold back no longer; but climbing over the garden-fence, I crept forward, followed by D'Hauteville.

In a few seconds both of us had gained the desired position—directly in front of the window, from which we were now separated only by the wood-work of the verandah. Standing half-bent our eyes were on a level with the floor of the room. The curtain had not fallen properly into its place. A single pane of the glass remained unscreened, and through this we could see nearly the whole interior of the apartment. Our ears, too, were at the proper elevation to catch every sound; and persons conversing within the room we could hear distinctly.

We were right in our conjecture. It was Aurore we had seen. Gayarre was the other occupant of the room.

I shall not paint that scene. I shall not repeat the words to which we listened. I shall not detail the speeches of that mean villain—at first fulsome and flattering—then coarse, bold, and brutal; until at length, failing to effect his purpose by entreaties, he had recourse to threats.

D'Hauteville held me back, begging me in earnest whispers to be patient. Once or twice I had almost determined to spring forward, dash aside the sash, and strike the ruffian to the floor. Thanks to the prudent interference of my companion, I restrained myself.

The scene ended by Gayarre going out of the room indignant, but somewhat crestfallen. The bold upright bearing of the quadroon—whose strength, at least, equalled that of her puny assailant—had evidently intimidated him for the moment, else he might have resorted to personal violence.

His threats, however, as he took his departure, left no doubt of his intention soon to renew his brutal assault. He felt certain of his victim—she was his slave, and must yield. He had ample time and opportunity. He need not at once proceed to extremes.

He could wait until his valour, somewhat cowed, should return again, and imbue him with a fresh impulse.

The disappearance of Gayarre gave us an opportunity to make our presence known to Aurore. I was about to climb up to the verandah and tap on the glass; but my companion prevented me from doing so.

"It is not necessary," he whispered; "she certainly knows you will be here. Leave it to *her*. She will return to the window presently. Patience, Monsieur! a false step will ruin all. Remember the dogs!"

There was prudence in these counsels, and I gave way to them. A few minutes would decide; and we both crouched close, and watched the movements of the quadroon.

The apartment in which she was attracted our notice. It was not the drawing-room of the house, nor yet a bedroom. It was a sort of library or studio — as shelves filled with books, and a table, covered with papers and writing materials, testified. It was, no doubt, the office of the avocat, in which he was accustomed to do his writing.

Why was Aurore in that room? Such a question occurred to us; but we had little time to dwell upon it. My companion suggested that as they had just arrived, she may have been placed there while an apartment was being prepared for her. The voices of servants overhead, and the noise of furniture being moved over the floor, was what led him to make this suggestion; it was just as if a room was being set in order.

This led me into a new train of reflection. She might be suddenly removed from the library, and taken up stairs. It would then be more difficult to communicate with her. It would be better to make the attempt at once.

Contrary to the wish of D'Hauteville, I was about to advance forward to the window, when the movements of Aurore herself caused me to hesitate.

The door through which Gayarre had just made his exit was visible from where we stood. I saw the quadroon approach this with silent tread, as if meditating some design. Placing her hand upon the key, she turned it in the lock, so that the door was thus bolted inside. With what design had she done this?

It occurred to us that she was about to make her escape out by the window, and that she had fastened the door for the purpose of delaying pursuit. If so, it would be better for us to remain quiet, and leave her to complete the design. It would be time enough to warn her of our presence when she should reach the window. This was D'Hauteville's advice.

In one corner of the room stood a large mahogany desk, and over its head was ranged a screen of box-shelves—of the kind known as "pigeon-holes." These were filled with papers and parchments,—no doubt, wills, deeds, and other documents relating to the business of the lawyer.

To my astonishment, I saw the quadroon as soon as she had secured the door, hastily approach this desk, and stand directly in front of it—her eyes eagerly bent upon the shelves, as though she was in search of some document!

Such was in reality the case, for she now stretched forth her hand, drew a bundle of folded papers from the box, and after resting her eyes upon them for a moment, suddenly concealed them in the bosom of her dress!

"Heavens!" I mentally ejaculated, "what can it mean?"

I had no time to give way to conjectures —for in a second's time, Aurore had glided across the floor, and was standing in the window.

As she raised the curtain, the light

streamed full on the faces of myself and my companion, and at the first glance she saw us. A slight exclamation escaped her, but it was of joy, not surprise; and she suddenly checked herself.

The ejaculation was not loud enough to be heard across the room. The sash opened noiselessly—with silent tread the verandah was crossed—and in another moment my betrothed was in my arms! I lifted her over the balustrade, and we passed hastily along the walks of the garden.

The outer field was reached without any alarm having been given; and, directing ourselves between the rows of the canes, we speeded on towards the woods, that loomed up like a dark wall in the distance.

CHAPTER XI.

THE LOST MUSTANGS.

The lightning continued to play at intervals, and we had no difficulty in finding our way. We recrossed near the same place where we had entered the field; and, guiding ourselves along the fence, hurried on towards the thicket of pawpaws, where we had left our horses.

My design was to take to the road at once, and endeavour to reach the city before daybreak. Once there, I hoped to be able to keep concealed — both myself and my betrothed — until some opportunity offered of getting out to sea, or up the river to one of the free states. I never thought of taking to the woods. Chance had made me acquainted with a rare hiding-place, and no doubt we might have found concealment there for a time. The advantage of this had crossed my mind, but I did not entertain the idea for a moment. Such a refuge could be but temporary. We should have to flee from it in the end, and the difficulty of escaping from the country would be as great as ever. Either for victim or criminal there is no place of concealment so safe as the crowded haunts of the populous city; and in New Orleans—half of which consists of a "floating" population—incognito is especially easy to be preserved.

My design, therefore—and D'Hauteville approved it—was to mount our horses, and make direct for the city.

Hard work I had cut out for our poor animals, especially the one that should have to "carry double." Tough hacks they were, and had done the journey up cleverly enough, but it would stretch all their muscle to take us back before daylight.

Aided by the flashes, we wound our way, amid the trunks of the trees, until at length we came within sight of the pawpaw thicket—easily distinguished by the large oblong leaves of the *asiminiers*, which had a whitish sheen under the electric light. We hurried forward with joyful anticipation. Once mounted, we should soon get beyond the reach of pursuit.

" Strange the horses do not neigh, or give some sign of their presence! One would have thought our approach would have startled them. But no, there is no whimper, no hoof-stroke; yet we must be close to them now. I never knew of horses remaining so still. What can they be doing? Where are they?"

" Aye, where are they?" echoed D'Hauteville, " surely this is the spot where we left them?"

" Here it certainly was! Yes — here — this is the very sapling to which I fastened my bridle—See! here are their hoof-prints. By Heaven! the *horses are gone!*"

I uttered this with a full conviction of its truth. There was no room left for doubt. There was the trampled earth where they had stood — there the very tree to which we had tied them. I easily recognised it, —for it was the largest in the grove.

Who had taken them away? This was the question that first occurred to us. Some one had been dogging us? Or had it been some one who had come across the animals by accident? The latter supposition was the less probable. Who would have been wandering in the woods on such a night? or even if any one had, what would have taken them into the pawpaw thicket? Ha! a new thought came into my head—perhaps the horses had got loose of themselves?

That was likely enough. Well, we should be able to tell as soon as the lightning flashed again, whether they had set themselves free; or whether some human hand had undone the knotted bridles.

We stood by the tree waiting for the light.

It did not tarry long; and when it came it enabled us to solve the doubt. My conjecture was correct; the horses had freed themselves. The broken branches told the tale. Something—the lightning—or more likely a prowling wild beast, had *stampeded* them; and they had broken off into the woods.

We now reproached ourselves for having so negligently fastened them — for having tied them to a branch of the *asiminier*, whose soft succulent wood possesses scarcely the toughness of an ordinary herbaceous plant. I was rather pleased at the discovery that the animals had freed themselves. There was a hope they had not strayed far. We might yet find them near at hand, with trailing bridles, cropping the grass.

Without loss of time we went in search of them—D'Hauteville took one direction,

I another, while Aurore remained in the thicket of pawpaws.

I ranged around the neighbourhood, went back to the fence, followed it to the road, and even went some distance along the road. I searched every nook among the trees, pushed through thickets and canebrakes, and, whenever it flashed, examined the ground for tracks. At intervals I returned to the point of starting, to find that D'Hauteville had been equally unsuccessful.

After nearly an hour spent in this fruitless search, I resolved to give it up. I had no longer a hope of finding the horses; and, with despairing step, I turned once more in the direction of the thicket. D'Hauteville had arrived before me.

As I approached, the quivering gleam enabled me to distinguish his figure. He was standing beside Aurore. He was conversing familiarly with her. I fancied he was *polite* to her, and that she seemed pleased. There was something in this slight scene that made a painful impression upon me.

Neither had he found any traces of the missing steeds. It was no use looking any longer for them; and we agreed to discontinue the search, and pass the night in the woods.

It was with a heavy heart that I consented to this; but we had no alternative. Afoot we could not possibly reach New Orleans before morning; and to have been found on the road after daybreak would have insured our capture. Such as we could not pass without observation; and I had no doubt that, at the earliest hour, a pursuing party would take the road to the city.

Our most prudent plan was to remain all night where we were, and renew our search for the horses as soon as it became day. If we should succeed in finding them, we might conceal them in the swamp till the following night, and then make for the city. If we should not recover them, then, by starting at an earlier hour, we might attempt the journey on foot.

The loss of the horses had placed us in an unexpected dilemma. It had seriously diminished our chances of escape, and increased the peril of our position.

Peril I have said, and in such we stood— peril of no trifling kind. You will with difficulty comprehend the nature of our situation. You will imagine yourself reading the account of some ordinary lover's escapade — a mere runaway match, *à la Gretna Green.*

Rid yourself of this fancy. Know that all three of us had committed an act for which we were amenable. Know that my *crime* rendered me liable to certain and severe punishment by the *laws of the land;* that a still more terrible sentence might be feared *outside the laws of the land.* I knew all this—I knew that life itself was imperilled by the act I had committed!

Think of our danger, and it may enable you to form some idea of what were our feelings after returning from our bootless hunt after the horses.

We had no choice but stay where we were till morning.

We spent half-an-hour in dragging the *tillandsia* from the trees, and collecting the soft leaves of the pawpaws. With these I strewed the ground; and, placing Aurore upon it, I covered her with my cloak.

For myself I needed no couch. I sat down near my beloved, with my back against the trunk of a tree. I would fain have pillowed her head upon my breast, but the presence of D'Hauteville restrained me. Even that might not have hindered me, but the slight proposal which I made had been declined by Aurore. Even the hand that I had taken in mine was respectfully withdrawn!

I will confess that this coyness surprised and piqued me.

CHAPTER XII.

A NIGHT IN THE WOODS.

Lightly clad as I was, the cold dews of the night would have prevented me from sleeping; but I needed not that to keep me awake. I could not have slept upon a couch of eider.

D'Hauteville had generously offered me his cloak, which I declined. He, too, was clad in cottonade and linen—though that was not the reason for my declining his offer. Even had I been suffering, I could not have accepted it. I began to fear him!

Aurore was soon asleep. The lightning showed me that her eyes were closed, and I could t... by her soft regular breathing that she slept. This, too, annoyed me!

I watched for each new gleam that I might look upon her. Each time as the quivering light illumined her lovely features, I gazed upon them with mingled feelings of passion and pain. Oh! could there be falsehood under that fair face? Could sin exist in that noble soul? After all, was I *not* beloved?

Even so, there was no withdrawing now—no going back from my purpose. The race in which I had embarked must be run to the end—even at the sacrifice both of heart and life. I thought only of the purpose that had brought us there.

As my mind became calmer, I again reflected on the means of carrying it out. As soon as day should break, I would go in search of the horses—track them, if possible, to where they had strayed—recover them, and then remain concealed in the woods until the return of another night.

Should we not recover the horses, what then?

For a long time, I could not think of what was best to be done in such a contingency.

At length an idea suggested itself — a plan so feasible that I could not help communicating it to D'Hauteville, who like myself was awake. The plan was simple enough, and I only wondered I had not thought of it sooner. It was that he (D'Hauteville) should proceed to Bringiers, procure other horses or a carriage there, and at an early hour of the following night meet us on the Levee Road.

What could be better than this? There would be no difficulty in his obtaining the horses at Bringiers — the carriage more likely. D'Hauteville was not known—at least no one would suspect his having any relations with me. I was satisfied that the disappearance of the quadroon would be at once attributed to me. Gayarre himself would know that; and therefore I alone would be suspected and sought after·

D'Hauteville agreed with me that this would be the very plan to proceed upon, in case our horses could not be found; and having settled the details, we awaited with less apprehension for the approach of day.

* * * * *

Day broke at length. The grey light slowly struggled through the shadowy tree-tops, until it became clear enough to enable us to renew the search.

Aurore remained upon the ground; while D'Hauteville and I, taking different directions, set out after the horses.

D'Hauteville went farther into the woods, while I took the opposite route.

I soon arrived at the zigzag fence bounding the fields of Gayarre; for we were still upon the very borders of his plantation. On reaching this, I turned along its edge, and kept on for the point where the bye-road entered the woods. It was by this we had come in on the previous night, and I thought it probable the horses might have taken it into their heads to stray back the same way.

I was right in my conjecture. As soon as I entered the embouchure of the road, I espied the hoof-tracks of both animals going out towards the river. I saw also those we had made on the previous night coming in. I compared them. The tracks leading both ways were made by the same horses. One had a broken shoe, which enabled me at a glance to tell they were the same. I noted another "sign" upon the trail. I noted that our horses in passing out dragged their bridles, with branches adhering to them. This confirmed the original supposition, that they had broken loose.

It was now a question of how far they had gone. Should I follow and endeavour to overtake them? It was now bright daylight, and the risk would be great. Long before this, Gayarre and his friends would be up and on the alert. No doubt parties were already traversing the Levee Road as well as the bye-paths among the plantations. At every step I might expect to meet either a scout or a pursuer.

The tracks of the horses showed they had been travelling rapidly and straight onward. They had not stopped to browse. Likely they had gone direct to the Levee Road, and turned back to the city. They were livery horses, and no doubt knew the road well. Besides they were of the Mexican breed— "mustangs." With these lively animals the trick of returning over a day's journey without their riders is not uncommon.

To attempt to overtake them seemed hopeless as well as perilous, and I at once gave up the idea and turned back into the woods.

As I approached the pawpaw thicket, I walked with lighter tread. I am ashamed to tell the reason. Foul thoughts were in my heart.

The murmur of voices fell upon my ear.

"By heaven! D'Hauteville has again got back before me!"

I struggled for some moments with my honour. It gave way; and I made my further approach among the pawpaws with the silence of a thief.

"D'Hauteville and she in close and friendly converse! They stand fronting each other. Their faces almost meet—their attitudes betoken a mutual interest. They talk in an earnest tone—in the low murmuring of lovers! O God!"

At this moment the scene on the wharf-boat flashed on my recollection. I remembered the youth wore a cloak, and that he was of low stature. It was he who was standing before me! That puzzle was explained. I was but a waif—a foil—a thing for a coquette to play with!

There stood the *true* lover of Aurore!

I stopped like one stricken. The sharp aching of my heart, oh! I may never describe. It felt as if a poisoned arrow had pierced to its very core, and there remained fixed and rankling. I felt faint and sick. I could have fallen to the ground.

"She has taken something from her bosom. She is handing it to him! A love-token—a *gage d'amour!*

"No. I am in error. It is the parchment—the paper taken from the desk of the avocat. What does it mean? What mystery is this? Oh! I shall demand a full explanation from both of you. I shall —patience, heart!—patience!

"D'Hauteville has taken the papers, and hidden them under his cloak. He turns away. His face is now towards me. His eyes are upon me. I am seen!"

"Ho! Monsieur?" he inquired, advancing to meet me. "What success? You have seen nothing of the horses!"

I made an effort to speak calmly.

"Their tracks," I replied.

Even in this short phrase my voice was

quivering with emotion. He might easily have noticed my agitation, and yet he did not seem to do so.

"Only their tracks, Monsieur! Whither did they lead?"

"To the Levee Road. No doubt they have returned towards the city. We need have no farther dependence on them."

"Then I shall go to Bringiers at once?"

This was put hypothetically.

The proposal gave me pleasure. I wished him away.

I wished to be alone with Aurore.

"It would be as well," I assented, "if you do not deem it too early?"

"Oh, no! besides I have business in Bringiers that will occupy me all the day."

"Ah!"

"Doubt not my return to meet you. I am certain to procure either horses or a carriage. Half-an-hour after twilight you will find me at the end of the bye-road. Fear not, Monsieur! I have a strong presentiment that for you all will yet be well. For *me*—ah!"

A deep sigh escaped him as he uttered the last phrase.

What did it mean? Was he mocking me? Had this strange youth a secret beyond *my* secret? Did he *know* that Aurore loved *him?* Was he so confident—so sure of her heart, that he recked not thus leaving her alone with me? Was he playing with me as the tiger with its victim? Were *both* playing with me?

These horrid thoughts crowding up, prevented me from making a definite rejoinder to his remarks. I muttered something about hope, but he seemed hardly to heed my remark. For some reason he was evidently desirous of being gone; and bidding Aurore and myself adieu, he turned abruptly off, and with quick light steps, threaded his way through the woods.

With my eyes I followed his retreating form, until it was hidden by the intervening branches. I felt relief that he was gone. I could have wished that he was gone for ever. Despite the need we had of his assistance—despite the absolute necessity for his return—at that moment I could have wished that we should never see him again !

CHAPTER XIII.

LOVE'S VENGEANCE.

Now for an explanation with Aurore! Now to give vent to the dire passion of jealousy —to relieve my heart with recriminations— with the bitter-sweet vengeance of reproach!

I could stifle the foul emotion no longer —no longer conceal it. It must have expression in words.

I had purposely remained standing with my face averted from her, till D'Hauteville was gone out of sight. Longer too. I was endeavouring to still the wild throbbings of my breast—to affect the calmness of indifference. Vain hypocrisy! To her eyes my spite must have been patent, for in this the keen instincts of woman are not to be baffled.

It was even so. She comprehended all. Hence the wild act—the *abandon* to which at that moment she gave way.

I was turning to carry out my design, when I felt the soft pressure of her body against mine—her arms encircled my neck—her head, with face upturned, rested upon my bosom, and her large lustrous eyes sought mine with a look of melting inquiry!

That look should have satisfied me. Surely no eyes but the eyes of love could have borne such expression?

And yet I was not content. I faltered out,—

"Aurore, you do not love me!"

"*Ah! Monsieur, pourquoi cette cruauté? Je t'aime—mon Dieu! avec tout mon cœur je t'aime!*"

Even this did not still my suspicious thoughts. The circumstances had been too strong—jealousy had taken too firm a hold to be plucked out by mere assurances. Explanation alone could satisfy me. That or confession.

Having made a commencement, I went on. I detailed what I had seen at the landing—the after conduct of D'Hauteville—what I had observed the preceding night—what I had just that moment witnessed. I detailed all. I added no reproaches. There was time enough for them when I should receive her answer.

It came in the midst of tears. She had known D'Hauteville before—that was acknowledged. There *was* a mystery in the relations that existed between them. I was solicited not to require an explanation. My patience was appealed to. It was not her secret. I should soon know all. In due time all would be revealed.

How readily my heart yielded to these delicious words! I no longer doubted. How could I with those large eyes, full of love-light, shining through the tear-bedewed lashes?

My heart yielded. Once more my arms closed affectionately around the form of my betrothed, and a fervent kiss renewed the vow of our betrothal.

* * * * *

We could have remained long upon this love-hallowed spot, but prudence prompted us to leave it. We were too near to the point of danger. At the distance of two hundred yards was the fence that separated Gayarre's plantation from the wild woods; and from that could even be seen the house itself, far off over the fields. The thicket concealed us, it was true; but should pursuit lead that way, the thicket would be the first place that would be searched. It would be necessary to seek a hiding-place farther off in the woods.

I bethought me of the flowery glade—the scene of my adventure with the *crotalus*. Around it the underwood was thick and shady, and there were spots where we could remain screened from the observation of the keenest eyes. At that moment I thought only of such concealment. It never entered my head that there were means of discovering us, even in the heart of the tangled thicket, or the pathless maze of the canebrake. I resolved, therefore, to make at once for the glade.

The pawpaw thicket, where we had passed the night, lay near the south-eastern angle of Gayarre's plantation. To reach the glade it would be necessary for us to pass a mile or more to the northward. By taking a diagonal line through the woods, the chances were ten to one we should lose our way, and perhaps not find a proper place of concealment. The chances were, too, that we might not find a path, through the network of swamps and bayous that traversed the forest in every direction.

I resolved, therefore, to skirt the plantation, until I had reached the path that I had before followed to the glade, and which I now remembered. There would be some risk until we had got to the northward of Gayarre's plantation; but we should keep at a distance from the fence, and as much as possible in the underwood. Fortunately a belt of "palmetto" land, marking the limits of the annual inundation, extended northward through the woods, and parallel to the line of fence. This singular vegetation, with its broad fan-like fronds, formed an excellent cover; and a person passing through it with caution could not be observed from any great distance. The partial lattice-work of its leaves was rendered more complete by the tall flower-stalks of the *altheas*, and other malvaceous plants that shared the ground with the palmettoes.

Directing ourselves within the selvage of this rank vegetation, we advanced with caution; and soon came opposite the place, where we had crossed the fence on the preceding night. At this point the woods approached nearest to the house of Gayarre. As already stated, but one field lay between, but it was nearly a mile in length. It was dead level, however, and did not appear half so long. By going forward to the fence, we could have seen the house at the opposite end, and very distinctly.

I had no intention of gratifying my curiosity at that moment by such an act, and was moving on, when a sound fell upon my ear that caused me suddenly to halt, while a thrill of terror ran through my veins.

My companion caught me by the arm, and looked inquiringly in my face.

A caution to her to be silent was all the reply I could make; and, leaning a little lower, so as to bring my ear nearer to the ground, I listened.

The suspense was short. I heard the sound again. My first conjecture was right. It was the "gowl" of a hound!

There was no mistaking that prolonged and deep-toned note. I was too fond a disciple of St. Hubert not to recognise the bay of the long-eared molossian. Though distant and low, like the hum of a forest bee, I was not deceived in the sound. It fell upon my ears with a terrible import!

And why terrible was the baying of a hound? To me above all others, whose ears, attuned to the "tally ho!" and the "view hilloa!" regarded these sounds as the sweetest of music? Why terrible? Ah! you must think of the circumstances in which I was placed—you must think, too, of the hours I spent with the snake-charmer—of the tales he told me in that dark tree-cave —the stories of runaways, of sleuth-dogs, of man-hunters, and "nigger-hunts,"—practices long thought to be confined to Cuba, but which I found as rife upon the soil of Louisiana,—you must think of all these, and then you will understand why I trembled at the distant baying of a hound.

The howl I heard was still very distant. It came from the direction of Gayarre's house. It broke forth at intervals. It was not like the utterance of a hound upon the trail, but that of dogs just cleared from the kennel, and giving tongue to their joy at the prospect of sport.

Fearful apprehensions were stirred within me at the moment. A terrible conjecture rushed across my brain. *They were after us with hounds!*

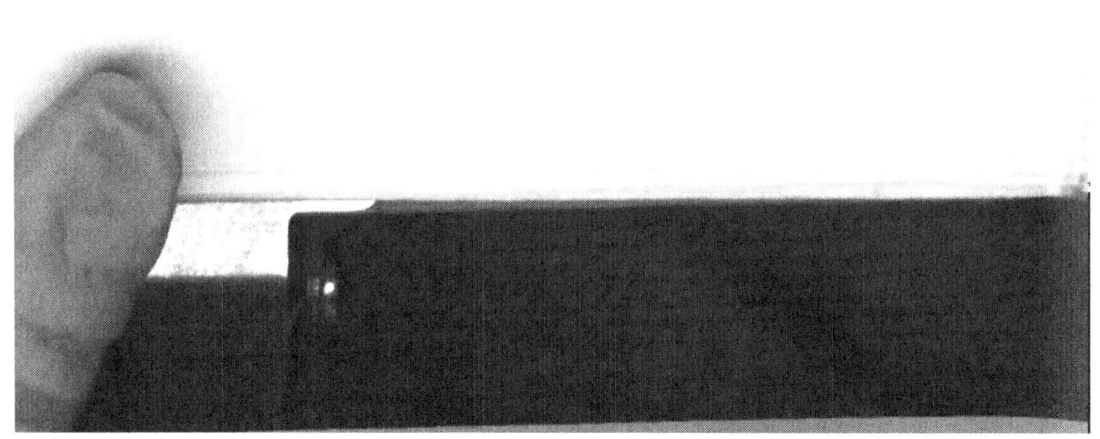

CHAPTER XIV.

HOUNDS ON OUR TRAIL.

O God! after us with hounds!

Either after us, or about to be, was the hypothetic form of my conjecture.

I could proceed no farther upon our path till I had become satisfied.

Leaving Aurore among the palmettoes, I ran directly forward to the fence, which was also the boundary of the woods. On reaching this, I grasped the branch of a tree, and swung myself up to such an elevation as would enable me to see over the tops of the cane. This gave me a full view of the house shining under the sun that had now risen in all his splendour.

At a glance I saw that I had guessed

aright. Distant as the house was, I could plainly see men around it, many of them on horseback. Their heads were moving above the canes; and now and then the deep bay of hounds told that several dogs were loose about the enclosure. The scene was just as if a party of hunters had assembled before going out upon a deer "drive;" and but for the place, the time, and the circumstances that had already transpired, I might have taken it for such. Far different, however, was the impression it made upon me. I knew well why was that gathering around the house of Gayarre. I knew well the game they were about to pursue.

I lingered but a moment upon my perch—long enough to perceive that the *hunters* were all mounted and ready to start.

With quick-beating pulse I retraced my steps; and soon rejoined my companion, who stood awaiting me with trembling apprehension.

I did not need to tell her the result of my reconnoissance : she read it in my looks. She, too, had heard the baying of the dogs. She was a native, and knew the customs of the land: she knew that hounds were used to hunt deer and foxes and wild cats of the woods; but she knew also that on many plantations there were some kept for a far different purpose—sleuth-dogs, *trained to the hunting of men!*

Had she been of slow comprehension, I might have attempted to conceal from her what I had learnt; but she was far from that, and with quick instinct she divined all.

Our first feeling was that of utter hopelessness. There seemed no chance of our escaping. Go where we would, hounds, trained to the scent of a human track, could not fail to follow and find us. It would be of no use hiding in the swamp or the bush. The tallest sedge or the thickest underwood could not give us shelter from pursuers like these.

Our first feeling, then, was that of hopelessness—quickly followed by a half-formed resolve to go no farther, to stand our ground, and be taken. We had not death to fear; though I knew that if taken I might make up my mind to some rough handling. I knew the feeling that was abroad in relation to the Abolitionists—at that time raging like a fever. I had heard of the barbarous treatment which some of these "fanatics" —as they were called—had experienced at the hands of the incensed slave-owners. I should no doubt be reckoned in the same category, or maybe, still worse, be charged as a "nigger-stealer." In any case I had to fear chastisement, and of no light kind either.

But my dread of this was nothing when compared with the reflection that, if taken, *Aurore must go back to Gayarre!*

It was this thought more than any other that made my pulse beat quickly. It was this thought that determined me not to surrender until after every effort to escape should fail us.

I stood for some moments pondering on what course to pursue. All at once a thought came into my mind that saved me from despair. That thought was of Gabriel the runaway.

Do not imagine that I had forgotten him or his hiding-place all this time. Do not fancy I had not thought of him before. Often, since we had entered the woods, had he and his tree-cave arisen in my memory; and I should have gone there for concealment, but that the distance deterred me. As we intended to return to the Levee Road after sunset, I had chosen the glade for our resting-place, on account of its being nearer.

Even then, when I learnt that hounds would be after us, I had again thought of making for the Bambarra's hiding-place; but had dismissed the idea, because it occurred to me that *the hounds could follow us anywhere*, and that, by taking shelter with the runaway, we should only guide his tyrants upon *him*.

So quick and confused had been all these reflections, that it had never occurred to me that the hounds *could not trail us across water*. It was only at that moment, when pondering how I could throw them off the track—thinking of the snake-charmer and his pine-cones—that I remembered the water.

Sure enough, in that still lay a hope; and I could now appreciate the remarkable cunning with which the lair of the runaway had been chosen. It was just the place to seek refuge from " de dam blood-dogs."

The moment I thought of it, I resolved to flee thither.

I would be sure to know the way. I had taken especial pains to remember it; for even on the day of my snake-adventure, some half-defined thoughts — something more like a presentiment than a plan—had

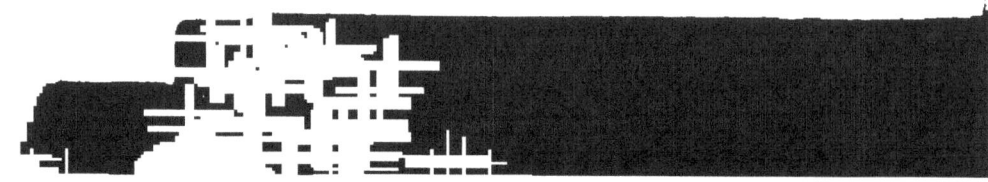

passed through my mind, vaguely pointing to a contingency like the present. Later events, and particularly my design of escaping to the city at once, had driven these thoughts out of my mind. For all that, I still remembered the way by which the Bambarra had guided me, and could follow it with hurried steps—though there was neither road nor path, save the devious tracks made by cattle or the wild animals of the forest.

But I was certain I knew it well. I should remember the signs and "blazes" to which the guide had called my attention. I should remember where it crossed the "big bayou" by the trunk of a fallen tree that served as a foot-bridge. I should remember where it ran through a strip of marsh impassable for horses, through the cane-brake, among the great knees and buttocks of the cypresses, down to the edge of the water. And that huge tree, with its prostrate trunk projecting out into the lake, and its moss-wrapped branches—that cunning harbour for the little pirogue—I should be sure to remember.

Neither had I forgotten the signal, by which I was to warn the runaway whenever I should return. It was a peculiar whistle he had instructed me to give, and also the number of times I was to utter it.

I had not waited for all these reflections. Many of them were after-thoughts, that occurred along the way. The moment I remembered the lake, I resolved upon my course; and, with a word of cheer to my companion, we again moved forward.

CHAPTER XV.

THE SIGNAL.

THE change in our plans made no change in the direction. We continued on in the same course. The way to the lake passed by the glade, where we had purposed going —indeed, through the middle of it lay the nearest path to the lair of the runaway.

Not far from the north-east angle of Gayarre's plantation, was the spot where I had parted with the black on the night of my adventure with him. It was at this point the path entered the woods. The blaze upon a sweet-gum tree, which I remembered well, showed me the direction. I was but too glad to turn off here, and leave the open woods; the more so that, just as we had reached the turning-point, the cry of the hounds came swelling upon the air, loud and prolonged. From the direction of the sound, I had no doubt but that they were already in the cane-field, and lifting our trail of the preceding night.

For a few hundred yards farther the timber was thin. The axe had been flourished there, as the numerous "stumps" testified. It was there the "firewood" was procured for the use of the plantation, and "cords" of it, already cut and piled, could be seen on both sides of our path. We passed among these with trembling haste. We feared to meet with some of the wood-cutters, or the driver of a wood-wagon. Such an encounter would have been a great misfortune; as, whoever might have seen us would have guided our pursuers on the track.

Had I reasoned calmly I would not have felt uneasiness on this head. I might have known, that if the dogs succeeded in tracking us thus far, they would need no direction from either wagoner or wood-chopper. But in the hurry of the moment I did not think of this; and I felt relief when we had passed through the tract of broken woods, and were entering under the more sombre shadow of the virgin forest.

It was now a question of time—a question of whether we should be able to reach the lake, summon the Bambarra with his pirogue, and be paddled out of sight, before the dogs should trail us to the edge of the water. Should we succeed in doing so, we should then have a fair prospect of escape. No doubt the dogs would guide our pursuers to the place of our embarkation—the fallen tree—but then both dogs and men would be at fault. That gloomy lake of the woods was a rare labyrinth. Though the open water was a surface of small extent, neither it, nor the island-like motte of timber in its centre, was visible from the place of embarkation; and, besides the lake itself, the inundation covered a large tract of the forest. Even should our pursuers be certain that we had escaped by the water, they might despair of finding us in the midst of such a maze — where the atmosphere at that season of full foliage had the hue of a dark twilight.

But they would hardly be convinced of our escape in that way. There was no trace left where the pirogue was moored— no mark upon the tree. They would scarce suspect the existence of a canoe in such an out-of-the-way spot, where the water—a mere stagnant pond—had no communication either with the river or the adjacent bayous. We were leaving no tracks—I took care of that—that could be perceived under the forest gloom; and our pursuers might possibly conclude that the dogs had been running upon the trail of a bear, a cougar, or the swamp wild-cat (*Lynx rufus*)—all of which animals freely take the water when pursued. With such probabilities I was cheering myself and my companion, as we kept rapidly along our course!

My greatest source of apprehension was the delay we should have to make, after giving the signal to the runaway. Would he hear it at once? Would he attend to it in due haste? Would he arrive in time? These were the points about which I felt chiefly anxious. Time was the important consideration; in that lay the conditions of our danger. Oh! that I had thought of this purpose before!—oh! that we had started earlier!

How long would it take our pursuers to come up? I could scarce trust myself to think of a reply to this question. Mounted as they were, they would travel faster than we: the dogs would guide them at a run!

One thought alone gave me hope. They would soon find our resting-place of the night; they would see where we had slept by the pawpaw-leaves and the moss; they could not fail to be certain of all that; but would they so easily trail us thence? In our search after the horses, we had tracked the woods in all directions. I had gone back to the bye-road, and some distance along it. All this would surely baffle the dogs for a while; besides, D'Hauteville, at starting, had left the pawpaw thicket by a different route from that we had taken. They might go off on *his* trail. Would that they might follow D'Hauteville!

All these conjectures passed rapidly through my mind as we hurried along. I even thought of making an attempt to throw the hounds off the scent. I thought of the *ruse* practised by the Bambarra with the spray of the loblolly pine; but, unfortunately, I could not see any of these trees on our way, and feared to lose time by going in search of one. I had doubts, too, of the efficacy of such a proceeding, though the black had solemnly assured me of it. The common red onion, he had afterwards told me, would be equally effective for the like purpose! But the red onion grew not in the woods, and the *pin de l'encens* I could not find.

For all that I did not proceed without precautions. Youth though I was, I was an old hunter, and had some knowledge of "woodcraft," gathered in deer-stalking, and in the pursuit of other game, among my native hills. Moreover, my nine months of New-world life had not all been passed within city walls; and I had already become initiated into many of the mysteries of the great American forest.

I did not proceed, then, in mere reckless haste. Where precautions could be observed, I adopted them.

A strip of marsh had to be crossed. It was stagnant water, out of which grew flags and the shrub called "swamp-wood" (*Bois de marais*). It was knee-deep, and could be waded. I knew this, for I had crossed it before. Hand in hand we waded through, and got safe to the opposite side; but on entering

I took pains to choose a place, where we stepped at once from the dry ground into the water. On going out, I observed a like precaution—so that our tracks might not appear in the mud.

Perhaps I should not have taken all this trouble, had I known that there were "hunters" among those who pursued us. I fancied the crowd I had seen were but planters, or people of the town—hurriedly brought together by Gayarre and his friends. I fancied they might not have much skill in tracking, and that my simple trick might be sufficient to mislead them.

Had I known that at their head was a man of whom Gabriel had told me much— a man *who made negro-hunting his profession*, and who was the most noted "tracker" in all the country—I might have saved myself both the time and the trouble I was taking. But I knew not that this ruffian and his trained dogs were after us, and I did my utmost to throw my pursuers off.

Shortly after passing the marsh, we crossed the "big bayou" by means of its tree-bridge. Oh! that I could have destroyed that log, or hurled it from its position. I consoled myself with the idea, that though the dogs might follow us over it, it would delay the pursuers awhile, who, no doubt, were all on horseback.

We now passed through the glade, but I halted not there. We stopped not to look upon its bright flowers—we perceived not their fragrance. Once I had wished to share this lovely scene in the company of Aurore. We were now in its midst, but under what circumstances! What wild thoughts were passing through my brain, as we hurried across this flowery tract under bright sunshine, and then plunged once more into the sombre atmosphere of the woods!

The path I remembered well, and was able to pursue it without hesitancy. Now and then only did I pause—partly to listen, and partly to rest my companion, whose bosom heaved quick and high with the rude exertion. But her glance testified that her courage was firm, and her smile cheered *me* on.

At length we entered among the cypress-trees that bordered the lake; and, gliding around their massive trunks, soon reached the edge of the water.

We approached the fallen tree; and climbing up, advanced along its trunk until we stood among its moss-covered branches.

I had provided myself with an instrument —a simple joint of the cane which grew plenteously around, and which with my knife I had shaped after a fashion I had been already taught by the Bambarra. With this I could produce a sound, that would be heard at a great distance off, and plainly to the remotest part of the lake.

Taking hold of the branches, I now bent down, until my face almost touched the surface of the water; and placing the reed to my lips, I gave utterance to the signal.

CHAPTER XVI.

THE SLEUTH-HOUNDS.

The shrill whistle, pealing along the water, pierced the dark aisles of the forest. It aroused the wild denizens of the lake, who, startled by such an unusual sound, answered it with their various cries in a screaming concert. The screech of the crane and the Louisiana heron, the hoarse hooting of owls, and the hoarser croak of the pelican, mingled together; and, louder than all, the scream of the osprey and the voice of the bald eagle—the last falling upon the ear with sharp metallic repetitions that exactly resembled the filing of saws.

For some moments this commotion was kept up; and it occurred to me that if I had to repeat the signal then it would not have been heard. Shrill as it was, it could scarce have been distinguished in such a din!

Crouching among the branches, we remained to await the result. We made no attempts at idle converse. The moments were too perilous for aught but feelings of extreme anxiety. Now and then a word of cheer—a muttered hope—were all the communications that passed between us.

With earnest looks we watched the water—with glances of fear we regarded the land. On one side we listened for the plashing of a paddle; on the other we dreaded to hear the "howl" of a hound. Never can I forget those moments—those deeply-anxious moments. Till death I may not forget them.

Every thought at the time—every incident, however minute—now rushes into my remembrance, as if it were a thing of yesterday.

I remember that once or twice, away

under the trees, we perceived a ripple along the surface of the water. Our hearts were full of hope—we thought it was the canoe.

It was a fleeting joy. The waves were made by the great saurian, whose hideous body—large almost as the pirogue itself—next moment passed before our eyes, cleaving the water with fish-like velocity.

I remember entertaining the supposition that the runaway *might not be in his lair*. He might be off in the forest—in search of food—or on any other errand. Then the reflection followed—if such were the case, I should have found the pirogue by the tree? Still he might have other landing-places around the lake—on the other side perhaps. He had not told me whether or no, and it was probable enough. These hypothetic conjectures increased my anxiety.

But there arose another, far more dreadful, because far more probable,—

The black might be asleep!

Far more probable, because night was

his day, and day his night. At night he was abroad, roaming and busy—by day he was at home and slept.

"Oh, Heavens! if he should be asleep, and not have heard the signal!"

Such was the terrible fancy that rushed across my brain.

I felt suddenly impelled to repeat the signal—though I thought at the time, if my conjecture were correct, there was but little hope he would hear me. A negro sleeps like a torpid bear. The report of a gun or a railway-whistle alone could awake one. There was no chance for a puny pipe like mine—the more especially as the screaming concert still continued.

"Even if he should hear it, he would hardly be able to distinguish the whistle from—— Merciful heavens!"

I was speaking to my companion when this exclamation interrupted me. It came from my own lips, but with involuntary utterance. It was called forth by a sound of dread import—a sound that I could hear above the shrill screaming of the birds, and hearing could interpret. It was the trumpet-like baying of a hound!

I stood bent, and listening,—I heard it again. There was no mistaking that note. I had the ears of a hunter. I knew the music well.

Oh! how unlike to music then! It fell upon my ears like a cry of vengeance—like a knell of death!

I thought no longer of repeating the signal; even if heard, it would be too late. I flung the reed away, as a useless toy. I drew Aurore along the tree, passing her behind me; and raising myself erect, stood fronting the land.

Again the "gowl" broke out—its loud echoes rolling through the woods—this time so near, that every moment I expected to see the animal that had uttered it.

I had not long to wait. A hundred yards off was a cane-brake. I could perceive a motion among the tall reeds. Their tops swayed to and fro, and their hollow culms rattled against each other, as they were jerked about, and borne downward. Some living thing was pressing through their midst.

The motion reached their verge—the last canes gave way, and I now saw what I had looked for—the spotted body of a hound! With a spring the animal came forth, paused for a moment in the open ground, and then, uttering a prolonged howl, took up the scent, and galloped forward.

Close upon his heels came a second; the waving cane closed behind them, and both ran forward in the direction of the log.

As there was no longer any underwood, I had a full view of their bodies. Gloomy as the place was, I could see them with sufficient distinctness to note their kind, —huge, gaunt deer-hounds, black and tan. From the manner of their approach, they had evidently been trained to their work, and that was *not* the hunting of deer. No ordinary hound would have run upon a human track, as they were running upon ours.

The moment I saw these dogs, I made ready for a conflict. Their huge size, their broad heavy jaws, and ferocious looks, told what savage brutes they were; and I felt satisfied they would attack me, as soon as they came up.

With this belief I drew forth a pistol; and, laying hold of a branch to steady me, I stood waiting their approach.

I had not miscalculated. On reaching the prostrate trunk, he scarcely made a pause; but, leaping upward, came running along the log. He had dropped the scent, and now advanced with eyes glaring, evidently meditating to spring upon me.

My position could not have been better, had I spent an hour in choosing it. From the nature of the ground, my assailant could neither dodge to the right nor the left; but was compelled to approach me in a line as straight as an arrow. I had nought to do but hold my weapon firm and properly directed. A novice with fire-arms could hardly have missed such an object.

My nerves were strung with anger—a feeling of intense indignation was burning in my breast, that rendered me as firm as steel. I was cool from very passion—at the thought of being thus hunted like a wolf!

I waited until the muzzle of the hound almost met that of the pistol, and then I fired. The dog tumbled from the log.

I saw the other close upon his heels. I aimed through the smoke, and again pulled trigger.

The good weapon did not fail me. Again the report was followed by a plunge.

The hounds were no longer upon the log. They had fallen right and left into the black water below!

CHAPTER XVII.

THE MAN-HUNTER.

The hounds had fallen into the water—one dead, the other badly wounded. The latter could not have escaped as one of his legs had been struck by the bullet, and his efforts to swim were but the throes of desperation. In a few minutes he must have gone to the bottom; but it was not his fate to die by drowning. It was predestined that his howling should be brought to a termination in a far different manner.

The voice of the dog is music to the ear of the alligator. Of all other animals, this is the favourite prey of the great saurian; and the howl of hound or cur will attract him from any distance where it may be heard.

Naturalists have endeavoured to explain this in a different way. They say—and such is the fact—that the howling of a dog bears a resemblance to the voice of the young alligator, and that the old ones are attracted towards the spot where it is heard—the mother to protect, and the male parent to devour it!

This is a disputed point in natural history; but there can be no dispute that the alligator eagerly preys upon the dog whenever an opportunity offers—seizing the canine victim in his terrible jaws, and carrying it off to his aqueous retreat. This he does with an air of such earnest avidity, as to leave no doubt but that he esteems the dog a favourite morsel.

I was not surprised, then, to see half-a-dozen of these gigantic reptiles emerging from amid the dark tree-trunks, and hastily swimming towards the wounded hound.

The continued howling of the latter guided them; and in a few seconds they had

surrounded the spot where he struggled, and were dashing forward upon their victim.

A shoal of sharks could not have finished him more expeditiously. A blow from the tail of one silenced his howling—three or four pair of gaunt jaws closed upon him at the same time—a short scuffle ensued—then the long bony heads separated, and the huge reptiles were seen swimming off again—each with a morsel in his teeth. A few bubbles and blotches of red froth mottling the inky surface of the water, were all that remained where the hound had lately been plunging.

Almost a similar scene occurred on the opposite side of the log—for the water was but a few feet in depth, and the dead hound was visible as he lay at the bottom. Several of the reptiles approaching on that side, had seen this one at the same time, and, rushing forward, they served him precisely as his companion had been served by the others. A crumb of bread could not have disappeared sooner among a shoal of hungry minnows, than did the brace of deer-hounds down the throats of these ravenous reptiles.

Singular as was the incident, it had scarce drawn my notice. I had far other things to think of.

After firing the pistol, I remained standing upon the tree, with my eyes fixed in the direction whence came the hounds.

I gazed intently among the tree-trunks, away up the dark vistas of the forest. I watched the cane-brake, to note the slightest motion in the reeds. I listened to every sound, while I stood silent myself, and enjoined silence upon my trembling companion.

I had but little hope then. There would be more dogs, no doubt — slower hounds following in the distance—and with them the mounted man-hunters. They could not be far behind — they could not fail to come up soon—the sooner that the report of my pistol would guide them to the spot. It would be of no use making opposition to a crowd of angry men. I could do nothing else than surrender to them.

My companion entreated me to this course; abjured me not to use my weapons—for I now held the second pistol in my hand. But I had no intention of using them should the crowd of men come up; I had only taken out the pistol as a precaution against the attack of the dogs—should any more appear.

For a good while I heard no sounds from the forest, and saw no signs of our pursuers. What could be detaining them? Perhaps the crossing of the bayou, or the tract of marsh. I knew the horsemen must there leave the trail; but were they all mounted?

I began to hope that Gabriel might yet be in time. If he had not heard the signal-whistle, he must have heard the reports of my pistol? But, on second thoughts, that might only keep him back. He would not understand the firing, and might fear to come with the pirogue!

Perhaps he had heard the first signal, and was now on his way. It was not too late to entertain such a supposition. Notwithstanding what had passed, we had been yet but a short while upon the spot. If on the way, he might think the shots were fired from my double-barrelled gun — fired at some game. He might not be deterred. There was still a hope he might come in time. If so, we would be able to reach his tree-cave in safety.

There was no trace of the dogs, save a blotch or two of blood upon the rough bark of the log, and that was not visible from the shore. Unless there were other dogs to guide them to the spot, the men might not in the darkness so easily discover these marks. We might yet baffle them!

With fresh hope, I turned once more towards the water, and gazed in the direction in which I expected the pirogue to come.

Alas! there was no sign of it. No sound came from the lake save the wild calling of the affrighted birds.

I turned once more to the land.

I saw the cane-brake in motion. The tall culms vibrated and crackled under the heavy tread of a man, who the next moment emerging into the open ground, advanced at a slinging trot towards the water!

He was alone and a-foot — there were no dogs with him — but the long rifle poised upon his shoulder, and the hunting accoutrements around his body, told me at a glance he was the owner of the deer-hounds.

His black bushy beard, his leggings, and buckskin shirt, his red neckcloth and raccoon cap — but above all, the brutal ferocity of his visage, left me in no doubt as to who this character was. The description of the runaway answered him in every particular. He could be no other than *Ruffin the man-hunter!*

CHAPTER XVIII.

SHOT FOR SHOT.

YES, the individual who now advanced was Ruffin the man-hunter; and the dogs I had killed were his — a brace of sleuth-hounds, well known in the settlement as being specially trained to tracking the unfortunate blacks, that, driven by cruel treatment, had taken to the woods.

Well known, too, was their master; a dissipated brutal fellow — half hunter, half hog-thief, who dwelt in the woods like an Indian savage, and hired himself out to such of the planters as needed the aid of him and his horrid hounds!

As I have said, I had never seen this individual, though I had heard of him often

—from Scipio, from the boy Caton, and, lastly, from Gabriel. The Bambarra had described him minutely—had told me wild stories of the man's wickedness and ferocious cruelty—how he had taken the lives of several runaways while in pursuit of them, and caused others to be torn and mangled by his savage dogs!

He was the terror and aversion of every negro quarter along the coast; and his name—appropriate to his character—oft served the sable mother as a "bogey" to frighten her squalling piccaninny into silence!

Such was Ruffin the *man-hunter*, as he was known among the black helots of the plantations. The "cobbing-board" and the red cowhide were not half so terrible as he. In comparison with him, such characters as "Bully Bill," the flogging overseer, might be esteemed mild and humane.

The sight of this man at once deprived

me of all farther thought of escape. I permitted my pistol arm to drop loosely by my side, and stood awaiting his advance, with the intention of surrendering ourselves up. Resistance would be vain, and could only lead to the idle spilling of blood. With this intention I remained silent, having cautioned my companion to do the same.

On first emerging from the cane-brake, the hunter did not see us. I was partially screened by the moss where I stood — Aurore entirely so. Besides, the man's eyes were not turned in our direction. They were bent upon the ground. No doubt he had heard the reports of my pistol; but he trusted more to his tracking instincts; and, from his bent attitude, I could tell that he was trailing his own dogs — almost as one of themselves would have done!

As he neared the edge of the pond, the *smell* of the water reached him; and, suddenly halting, he raised his eyes and looked forward. The sight of the pond seemed to puzzle him, and his astonishment was expressed in the short sharp expression,—

" H—ll ! "

The next moment his eyes fell upon the prostrate tree, then quickly swept along its trunk, and rested full upon me.

" H—ll and scissors ! " he exclaimed, " thar are ye ! Whar's my dogs ? "

I stood eyeing him back, but made no reply.

" You hear, d—n yer ! Whar's my dogs ? "

I still remained silent.

His eyes fell upon the log. He saw the blood-spots upon the bark. He remembered the shots.

" H—l and d—n ! " cried he, with horrid emphasis, " you've kilt my dogs ! " and then followed a volley of mingled oaths and threats, while the ruffian gesticulated as if he had suddenly gone mad !

After a while he ceased from these idle demonstrations; and, planting himself firmly, he raised his rifle muzzle towards me, and cried out:—

"Come off that log, and fetch yur blue-skin with you! Quick, d—n yer! Come off that log! Another minnit, an' I'll plug ye!"

I have said that at first sight of the man I had given up all idea of resistance, and intended to surrender at once; but there was something so arrogant in the demand—so insulting in the tone with which the ruffian made it—that it fired my very flesh with indignation, and determined me to stand at bay.

Anger, at being thus hunted, new-nerved both my heart and my arm. The brute had bayed me, and I resolved to risk resistance.

Another reason for changing my determination—I now saw that he was *alone*. He had followed the dogs afoot, while the others on horseback had no doubt been stopped or delayed by the bayou and morass. Had the crowd come up, I must have yielded *nolens volens;* but the man-hunter himself—formidable antagonist though he appeared—was still but *one*, and to surrender tamely to a single individual, was more than my spirit—inherited from border ancestry—could brook. There was too much of the moss-trooper blood in my veins for that, and I resolved, *coute que coute*, to risk the encounter.

My pistol was once more firmly grasped; and looking the ruffian full into his bloodshot eyes, I shouted back,—

"Fire at your peril! Miss and you are mine!"

The sight of my uplifted pistol caused him to quail; and I have no doubt that had opportunity offered, he would have withdrawn from the contest. He had expected no such a reception.

But he had gone too far to recede. His rifle was already at his shoulder, and the next moment I saw the flash, and heard the sharp crack. The "thud" of his bullet, too, fell upon my ear, as it struck into the branch against which I was leaning. Good marksman as he was reputed, the sheen of my pistols had spoiled his aim, and he had missed me!

I did not miss *him*. He fell to the shot with a demoniac howl; and as the smoke thinned off, I could see him writhing and scrambling in the black mud!

I hesitated whether to give him the second barrel—for I was angry and desired his life—but at this moment noises reached me from behind. I heard the plunging paddle, with the sounds of a manly voice; and turning, I beheld the Bambarra.

The latter had shot the pirogue among the tree-tops close to where we stood, and with voice and gesture now urged us to get aboard.

"Quick, mass'. Quick, 'Rore gal! jump into de dug-out! Jump in! Truss Ole

Gabe!—he stand by young mass' to de deff!"

Almost mechanically I yielded to the solicitations of the runaway—though I now saw but little chance of our ultimate escape—and, having assisted Aurore into the pirogue, I followed and took my seat beside her.

The strong arm of the negro soon impelled us far out from the shore; and in five minutes after we were crossing the open lake toward the cypress clump in its midst.

CHAPTER XIX.

LOVE IN THE HOUR OF PERIL.

We glided into the shadow of the tree, and passed under its trailing parasites. The pirogue touched its trunk. Mechanically I climbed along the sloping buttress—mechanically assisted Aurore.

We stood within the hollow chamber—the lurking-place of the runaway—and for the present were safe from pursuit. But there was no joy in our hearts. We knew it was but a respite, without any hope of ultimate concealment.

The encounter with Ruffin had ruined all our prospects. Whether the hunter were yet dead or alive, his presence would guide the pursuit. The way we had got off would easily be conjectured, and our hiding-place could not long remain undiscovered.

What had passed would be likely to aggravate our pursuers, and strengthen their determination to capture us. Before Ruffin came up, there was yet a chance of safety. Most of those engaged in the pursuit, would regard it as the mere ordinary affair of a chase after a runaway negro — a sport of which they might get tired whenever they should lose the track. Considering for whom the hunt was got up—a man so unpopular as Gayarre,—none would have any great interest in the result, excepting himself and his ruffian aids. Had we left no traces where we embarked in the pirogue, the gloomy labyrinth of forest-covered water might have discouraged our pursuers—most of whom would have given up at the doubtful prospect, and returned to their homes. We might have been left undisturbed until nightfall, and it was my design to have then recrossed the lake, landed at some new point, and, under the guidance of the Bambarra, get back to the Levee Road, where we were to meet D'Hauteville with the horses. Thence, as originally agreed upon, to the city.

All this programme, I had hastily conceived; and previous to the appearance of Ruffin, there was every probability I should succeed in carrying it out.

Even after I had shot the dogs, I did not wholly despair. There were still many chances of success that occurred to me. The pursuers, thought I, detained by the bayou, might have lost the dogs, and would not follow their track so easily. Some time would be wasted at all events. Even should they form a correct guess as to the fate of the hounds, neither men afoot nor on horseback could penetrate to our hiding-place. They would need boats or canoes. More time would be consumed in bringing these from the river, and perhaps night would be down before this could be effected. On night and D'Hauteville I still had confidence.

That was previous to the conflict with the man-hunter.

After that affair, circumstances had undergone a change. Alive or dead, Ruffin would guide the pursuit to where we were. If still living—and now that my angry feeling had passed away I hoped he was—he would at once direct the pursuers upon us.

I believed he was not dead — only wounded. His behaviour, after receiving the shot, had not been like that of a man mortally wounded. I believed, and hoped, that he still lived—not that I felt at all remorseful at what had happened, but from mere prudential considerations. If dead, his body by the prostrate tree would soon be discovered, and would tell the tale to those who came up. We should be captured all the same, and might expect the more terrible consequences.

The rencontre with this ruffian had been altogether unfortunate. It had changed the face of affairs. Blood had been spilt *in defence of a runaway*. The news would return rapidly to the town. It would spread through the plantations with lightning speed. The whole community would be fired and roused—the number of our pursuers quadrupled. I should be hunted as a *double* outlaw, and with the hostile energy of vengeance!

I knew all this, and no longer speculated upon the probabilities of deliverance. There was not the remotest prospect of our being able to get away.

I drew my betrothed near me. I folded her in my arms, and pressed her to my heart. Till death she would be mine! She swore it in that shadowy spot—in that dread and darksome hour. Till death she would be mine!

Her love inspired me with courage; and with courage I awaited the result.

* * * * *

Another hour passed.

Despite our fearful anticipations, that hour was pleasantly spent. Strange it is to say so, but it was in reality one of the happiest hours I can remember. It was the first time I had been enabled to hold free converse with Aurore, since the day of our betrothal. We were now alone — for the faithful black stood sentinel below by the hawser of his pirogue.

The reaction, consequent upon my late jealousy, had kindled my love to a renewed and fiercer life—for such is the law of nature. In the very ardour of my affection, I almost forgot our desperate situation.

Over and over again we vowed eternal troth—over and over plighted our mutual faith, in fond burning words—the eloquence of our heartfelt passion. Oh! it was a happy hour!

Alas! it came to an end. It ended with a painful regret, but not with surprise. I was not surprised to hear horns sounding through the woods, and signal shouts answering each other in different directions. I was not surprised when voices came pealing across the water, — loud oaths and ejaculations—mingled with the plashing of paddles and the plunging of oars; and, when the negro announced that several boats filled with armed men were in the open water and approaching the tree, it did not take me by surprise. I had foreseen all this.

I descended to the base of the cypress, and, stooping down, looked out under the hanging moss. I could see the surface of the lake. I could see the men in their canoes and skiffs, rowing and gesticulating.

When near the middle of the open water, they lay upon their oars, and held a short consultation. After a moment, they separated, and rowed in circles around, evidently with the design of encompassing the tree.

In a few minutes they had executed this

manœuvre, and now closed in, until their vessels floated among the drooping branches of the cypress. A shout of triumph told that they had discovered our retreat; and I now saw their faces peering through the curtain of straggling *tillandsia*.

They could see the pirogue, and both the negro and myself standing by the bow.

"Surrender!" shouted a voice in a loud firm tone. "If you resist, your lives be on your own heads!"

Notwithstanding this summons, the boats did not advance any nearer. They knew that I carried pistols, and that I knew how to handle them — the proofs were fresh. They approached, therefore, with caution — thinking I might still use my weapons.

They had no need to be apprehensive. I had not the slightest intention of doing so. Resistance against twenty men — for there were that number in the boats, twenty men well armed — would have been a piece of desperate folly. I never thought of such a thing; though, if I had, I believe the Bambarra would have stood by me to the death. The brave fellow, steeled to a supernatural courage by the prospect of his punishment, had even proposed fight! But his courage was madness; and I entreated him not to resist—as they would certainly have slain him upon the spot.

I meant no resistance, but I hesitated a moment in making answer.

"We're all armed," continued the speaker, who seemed to have some authority over the others. "It is useless for you to resist —you had better give up!"

"D—n them!" cried another and a rougher voice; "don't waste talk on them. Let's fire the tree, and smoke 'em out; that moss 'll burn, I reckon!"

I recognised the voice that uttered this inhuman suggestion. It came from Bully Bill.

"I have no intention of making resistance," I called out in reply to the first speaker. "I am ready to go with you. I have committed no crime. For what I have done I am ready to answer to the laws."

"You shall answer to *us*," replied one who had not before spoken; "*we* are the laws here."

There was an ambiguity in this speech that I liked not; but there was no further parley. The skiffs and canoes had suddenly closed in around the tree. A dozen muzzles of pistols and rifles were pointed at me, and a dozen voices commanded the negro and myself to get into one of the boats.

From the fierce determined glances of these rough men, I saw it was death or obedience.

I turned to bid adieu to Aurore, who had rushed out of the tree-cave, and stood near me weeping.

As I faced round, several men sprang upon the buttress; and, seizing me from behind, held me in their united grasp.

Then drawing my arms across my back, tied them fast with a rope.

I could just speak one parting word with Aurore, who, no longer in tears, stood regarding my captors with a look of scornful indignation. As they led me unresistingly into the boat, her high spirit gave way to words, and she cried out in a voice of scorn :—

"Cowards! Cowards! Not one of you dare meet him in a fair field—no, not one of you!"

The lofty spirit of my betrothed echoed mine, and gave me proof of her love. I was pleased with it, and could have applauded; but my mortified captors gave me no time to reply; for the next moment, the pirogue in which I had been placed shot out through the branches, and floated on the open water of the lake.

CHAPTER XX.

A TERRIBLE FATE.

I saw no more of Aurore. Neither was the black brought along. I could gather from the conversation of my captors, that they were to be taken in one of the skiffs that had stayed behind—that they were to be landed at a different point from that to which we were steering. I could gather, too, that the poor Bambarra was doomed to a terrible punishment—the same he already dreaded—the losing of an arm!

I was pained at such a thought, but still more by the rude jests I had now to listen to. My betrothed and myself were reviled with a disgusting coarseness, which I cannot repeat.

I made no attempt to defend either her or myself. I did not even reply. I sat with my eyes bent gloomily upon the water; and it was a sort of relief to me when the pirogue again passed in among the trunks of the cypress-trees, and their dark shadow half concealed my face from the view of my captors. I was brought back to the landing by the old tree-trunk.

On nearing this, I saw that a crowd of men awaited us on the shore; and among them I recognised the ferocious Ruffin, with his arm slung in his red kerchief, bandaged and bloody. He was standing up with the rest.

"Thank heaven! I have not killed him!" was my mental ejaculation. "So much the less have I to answer for."

The canoes and skiffs—with the exception of that which carried Aurore and the black—had all arrived at this point, and my captors were landing. In all there were some thirty or forty men, with a proportion of half-grown boys. Most of them were armed with either pistols or rifles. Under the grey gloom of the trees, they presented a picturesque tableau; but at that moment my feelings were not attuned to enjoy it.

I was landed among the rest; and with two armed men, one before and another immediately at my back, I was marched off through the woods. The crowd accompanied us, some in the advance, some behind, while others walked alongside. These were the boys and the more brutal of the men, who occasionally taunted me with rude speech.

I might have lost patience and grown angry, had that served me; but I knew it would only give pleasure to my tormentors, without bettering my condition. I therefore observed silence, and kept my eyes averted or turned upon the ground.

We passed on rapidly — as fast as the crowd could make way through the bushes —and I was glad of this. I presumed I was about to be conducted before a magistrate, or "justice of the peace," as there called. Well, thought I. Under legal authority, and in the keeping of the officers, I should be protected from the gibes and insults that were being showered upon me. Everything short of personal violence was offered; and there were some that seemed sufficiently disposed even for this.

I saw the forest opening in front. I supposed we had gone by some shorter way to the clearings. It was not so, for the next moment we emerged into the glade. Again the glade!

Here my captors came to a halt; and now in the open light I had an opportunity to know who they were. At a glance I saw that I was in the hands of a desperate crowd.

Gayarre himself was in their midst, and beside him his own overseer, and the negro-trader, and the brutal Larkin. With these were some half-dozen Creole Frenchmen of the poorer class of *proprietaires*,

weavers of cottonade, or small planters. The rest of the mob was composed of the very scum of the settlement — the drunken boatmen whom I had used to see gossiping in front of the "groceries," and other dissipated rowdies of the place. Not one respectable planter appeared upon the ground — not one respectable man!

For what had they stopped in the glade? I was impatient to be taken before the justice, and chafed at the delay.

"Why am I detained here?" I asked, in a tone of anger.

"Ho, mister!" replied one; "don't be in such a h—l of a hurry! Yu'll find out soon enough, I reckon."

"I protest against this," I continued. "I insist upon being taken before the justice."

"An' so ye will, d—n you! You hain't got fur to go. *The justice is hyar.*"

"Who? where?" I inquired, under the impression that a magistrate was upon the ground. I had heard of wood-choppers acting as justices of the peace—in fact, had met with one or two of them—and among the rude forms that surrounded me there might be one of these.

"Where is the justice?" I demanded.

"Oh, he's about—never you fear!" replied one.

"Whar's the justice?" shouted another.

"Aye, whar's the justice?—whar are ye, judge?" cried a third, as if appealing to some one in the crowd. "Come on hyar, judge!" he added. "Come along!—hyar's a fellar wants to see you!"

I really thought the man was in earnest. I really believed there was such an individual in the mob. The only impression made upon me was astonishment at this rudeness towards the magisterial representative of the law.

My misconception was short-lived, for at this moment Ruffin — the bandaged and bloody Ruffin—came close up to me; and, after scowling upon me with his fierce blood-shot eyes, bent forward until his lips almost touched my face, and then hissed out,—

"Perhaps, Mister nigger-stealer, you've niver heerd ov *Justice Lynch?*"

A thrill of horror ran through my veins. The fearful conviction flashed before my mind that *they were going to Lynch me!*

CHAPTER XXI.

THE SENTENCE OF JUDGE LYNCH.

An undefined suspicion of something of this sort had already crossed my thoughts. I remembered the reply made from the boats, " You shall answer to *us*. *We* are the law." I had heard some mysterious inuendoes as we passed through the woods — I had noticed, too, that on our arrival in the glade, we found those who had gone in the advance halted there, as if waiting for the others to come up; and I could not comprehend why we had stopped there at all.

I now saw that the men of the party were drawing to one side, and forming a sort of irregular ring, with that peculiar air of solemnity that bespeaks some serious business. It was only the boys, and some negroes—for these, too, had taken part in our capture—who remained near me. Ruffin had simply approached to gratify his revengeful feelings by tantalising me.

All these appearances had aroused wild suspicions within me, but up to that moment they had assumed no definite form. I had even endeavoured to keep back such a suspicion, under the vague belief, that by the very imagination of it, I might in some way aid in bringing it about!

It was no longer suspicion. It was now conviction. They were going to Lynch me!

The significant interrogatory, on account of the manner in which it was put, was hailed by the boys with a shout of laughter. Ruffin continued,—

"No; I guess you han't heerd ov that ar justice, since yur a stranger in these parts, an' a Britisher. You han't got sich a one among yur bigwigs, I reckin. He's the fellar that ain't a goin' to keep you long in Chancery. No, by G—d! he'll do yur business in double-quick time. H—l and scissors! yu'll see if he don't."

Throughout all this speech the brutal fellow taunted me with gestures as well as words—drawing from his auditory repeated bursts of laughter.

So provoked was I that, had I not been fast bound, I should have sprung upon him; but, bound as I was, and vulgar brute as was this adversary, I could not hold my tongue.

"Were I free, you ruffian, you would not dare taunt me thus. At all events *you* have come off but second best. I've crippled *you* for life; though it don't matter much, seeing what a clumsy use you make of a rifle."

This speech produced a terrible effect upon the brute — the more so that the boys now laughed at *him*. These boys were not all bad. They were incensed against me as an Abolitionist—or "nigger-stealer," as they phrased it—and, under the countenance and guidance of their elders, their worst passions were now at play; but, for all that, they were not essentially wicked. They were rough backwoods boys, and the spirit of my retort pleased them. After that they held back from jeering me.

Not so with Ruffin, who now broke forth into a string of vindictive oaths and menaces, and appeared as if about to grapple me with his one remaining hand. At this moment he was called off by the men, who needed him in the "caucus;" and, after shaking his fist in my face, and uttering a parting imprecation, he left me.

I was for some minutes kept in suspense. I could not tell what this dread council were debating, or what they meant to do with me—though I now felt quite certain that they did not intend taking me before any magistrate. From frequent phrases that reached my ears, such as, "flog the scoundrel," "tar and feathers," I began to conjecture that some such punishment awaited me. To my astonishment, however, I found, upon listening a while, that a number of my judges were actually opposed to these punishments as being too mild! Some declared openly, that *nothing but my life could satisfy the outraged laws!*

The *majority* took this view of the case; and it was to add to their strength that Ruffin had been summoned!

A feeling of terrible fear crept over me—say rather a feeling of horror—but it was only complete when the ring of men suddenly broke up, and I saw two of their number lay hold of a rope, and commence reeving it over the limb of a gum-tree that stood by the edge of the glade.

There had been a trial and a sentence too. Even Judge Lynch has his formality.

When the rope was adjusted, one of the men — the negro-trader it was — approached me; and in a sort of rude paraphrase of a judge, summed up and pronounced the sentence!

I had outraged the laws; I had committed two capital crimes. I had stolen slaves, and endeavoured to take away the life of a fellow-creature. A jury of twelve men had tried—and found me guilty; and sentenced me to death by hanging. Even this was not permitted to go forth in an informal manner. The very phraseology was adopted. I was to be hung by the neck until I should be dead—dead!

You will deem this relation exaggerated and improbable. You will think that I am sporting with you. You will not believe that such lawlessness can exist in a Christian — a civilised land. You will fancy that these men were sporting with *me*, and that in the end they did not seriously intend to *hang me*.

I cannot help it if you think so; but I solemnly declare that such was their design: and I felt as certain at that moment that they intended to have hanged me, as I now feel that I was not hanged!

Believe it or not, you must remember that I would not have been the first victim by many, and that thought was vividly before my mind at the time.

Along with it, there was the rope—there the tree—there stood my judges before me. Their looks alone might have produced conviction. There was not a ray of mercy to be seen!

At that awful moment I knew not what I said or how I acted.

I remember only that my fears were somewhat modified by my indignation. That I protested, menaced, swore—that my ruthless judges answered me with mockery.

They were actually proceeding to put the sentence into execution—and had already carried me across to the foot of the tree—when the sound of trampling hoofs fell upon our ears, and the next moment a party of horsemen galloped into the glade.

CHAPTER XXII.

IN THE HANDS OF THE SHERIFF.

At sight of these horsemen my heart leaped with joy, for among the foremost I beheld the calm resolute face of Edward Reigart. Behind him rode the sheriff of the parish, followed by a "posse" of about a dozen men—among whom I recognised several of the most respectable planters of the neighbourhood. Every one of the party was armed either with a rifle or pistols; and the manner in which they rode forward upon the ground, showed that they had come in great haste, and with a determined purpose.

I say my heart leaped with joy. An actual criminal standing upon the platform of the gallows could not have been more joyed at sight of the messenger that brought him reprief or pardon. In the new-comers I recognised friends. In their countenances I read rescue. I was not displeased, therefore, when the sheriff, dismounting, advanced to my side, and placing his hand upon my shoulder, told me I was his prisoner " in the name of the law." Though brusquely done, and apparently with a degree of rudeness, I was not displeased either by the act or the manner. The latter was plainly assumed for a purpose; and in the act itself I hailed the salvation of my life. I felt like a rescued man.

The proceeding did not equally content my former judges, who loudly murmured their dissatisfaction. They alleged that I had already been tried by a jury of *twelve free citizens*—that I had been found guilty of nigger-stealing — that I had stolen *two niggers*—that I had resisted when pursued, and had "wownded" one of my pursuers;

and that, as all this had been "clarly made out," they couldn't see what more was wanted to establish my guilt, and that I ought to be *hung* on the spot, without further loss of time.

The sheriff replied that such a course would be illegal; that the majesty of the law must be respected; that if I was guilty of the crimes alleged against me, the law would most certainly measure out full punishment to me; but that I must first be brought before a justice, and the charge legally and formally made out; and, finally, expressed his intention to take me before Justice Claiborne, the magistrate of the district.

An angry altercation ensued between the mob and the sheriff's party—in which but slight show of respect was paid to the high executive—and for some time I was actually in dread that the ruffians would carry their point. But an American sheriff is entirely a different sort of character from the idle gentleman who fills that office in an English county. The former is, in nine cases out of ten, a man of proved courage and action; and Sheriff Hickman, with whom my *quasi* judges had to deal, was no exception to this rule. His "posse," moreover, hurriedly collected by my friend Reigart, chanced to have among their number several men of a similar stamp. Reigart himself, though a man of peace, was well known to possess a cool and determined spirit; and there was the landlord of my hotel, and several of the planters who accompanied the sheriff—sterling men, who were lovers of the law and lovers of fair play as well—and those, armed to the teeth, would have laid down their lives on the spot in defence of the sheriff and his demand. True, they were in the minority in point of numbers; but they had the law upon their side, and that gave them strength.

There was one point in my favour above all others, and that was, my accusers chanced to be unpopular men. Gayarre, as already stated, although professing a high standard of morality, was not esteemed by the neighbouring planters — particularly by those of American origin. The others most forward against me, were known to be secretly instigated by the lawyer. As to Ruffin, whom I had " wownded," those upon the ground had heard the crack of his rifle, and knew that *he had fired first.* In their calmer moments my resistance would have been deemed perfectly justifiable — so far as that individual was concerned.

Had the circumstances been different— had the " two niggers " I had *stolen* belonged to a popular planter, and not to M. Dominique Gayarre — had Ruffin been a respectable citizen, instead of the dissipated half outlaw that he was — had there not been a suspicion in the minds of many present, that it was *not* a case of ordinary *nigger-stealing*, then indeed might it have gone ill with me, in spite of the sheriff and his party.

Even as it was, a long and angry altercation ensued — loud words, oaths, and gestures of menace, were freely exchanged — and both rifles and pistols were cocked and firmly grasped, before the discussion ended.

But the brave sheriff remained resolute; Reigart acted a most courageous part; my *ci-devant* host, and several of the young planters, behaved in a handsome manner; and the law prevailed.

Yes! thank Heaven and half-a-dozen noble men, the law prevailed—else I should never have gone out of that glade alive!

Justice Lynch had to give way to Justice Claiborne; and a respite was obtained from the cruel verdict of the former. The victorious sheriff and his party bore me off in their midst.

But though my ferocious judges had yielded for the present, it was not certain that they would not still attempt to rescue me from the hands of the law. To prevent this, the sheriff mounted me upon a horse —he himself riding upon one side, while an assistant of tried courage took the opposite. Reigart and the planters kept close to me before and behind; while the shouting blaspheming mob followed both on horseback and a-foot. In this way we passed through the woods, across the fields, along the road leading into Bringiers, and then to the residence of " Squire" Claiborne—Justice of the Peace for that district.

Attached to his dwelling was a large room or office where the Squire was used to administer the magisterial law of the land. It was entered by a separate door from the house itself; and had no particular marks about it to denote that it was a hall of justice, beyond the fact that it was furnished with a bench or two to serve as seats, and a small desk or rostrum in one corner.

At this desk the Squire was in the habit

of settling petty disputes, administering affidavits at a quarter of a dollar each, and arranging other small civic matters. But oftener was his magisterial function employed in sentencing the mutinous "darkie" to his due proportion of stripes on the complaint of a conscientious master—for, after all, such theoretical protection does the poor slave enjoy.

Into this room, then, was I hurried by the sheriff and his assistants—the mob rushing in after, until every available space was occupied.

CHAPTER XXIII.

THE CRISIS.

No doubt a messenger had preceded us; for we found Squire Claiborne in his chair of office, ready to hear the case. In the tall thin old man, with white hair and dignified aspect, I recognised a fit representative of justice—one of those venerable magistrates, who command respect not only by virtue of age and office, but from the dignity of their personal character. In spite of the noisy rabble that surrounded me, I read in the serene firm look of the magistrate the determination to show fair play.

I was no longer uneasy. On the way, Reigart had told me to be of good cheer. He had whispered something about "strange developments to be made;" but I had not fully heard him, and was at a loss to comprehend what he meant. In the hurry and crush, I had found no opportunity for an explanation.

"Keep up your spirits!" said he, as he pushed his horse alongside me. "Don't have any fear about the result. It's rather an odd affair, and will have an odd ending—rather unexpected for somebody, I should say—Ha! ha! ha!"

Reigart actually laughed aloud, and appeared to be in high glee! What could such conduct mean?

I was not permitted to know, for at that moment the sheriff, in a high tone of authority, commanded that no one should "hold communication with the prisoner;" and my friend and I were abruptly separated. Strange, I did not dislike the sheriff for this! I had a secret belief that his manner—apparently somewhat hostile to me—was assumed for a purpose. The mob required conciliation; and all this *brusquerie* was a bit of management on the part of Sheriff Hickman.

On arriving before Justice Claiborne, it required all the authority of both sheriff and justice to obtain silence. A partial lull, however, enabled the latter to proceed with the case.

"Now, gentlemen!" said he, speaking in a firm magisterial tone, "I am ready to hear the charge against this young man. Of what is he accused, Colonel Hickman?" inquired the justice turning to the sheriff.

"Of negro-stealing, I believe," replied the latter.

"Who prefers the charge?"

"Dominique Gayarre," replied a voice from the crowd, which I recognised as that of Gayarre himself.

"Is Monsieur Gayarre present?" inquired the justice.

The voice again replied in the affirmative; and the fox-like face of the avocat now presented itself in front of the rostrum.

"Monsieur Dominique Gayarre," said the magistrate, recognising him, "what is the charge you bring against the prisoner? State it in full and upon oath."

Gayarre having gone through the formula of the oath, proceeded with his plaint in true lawyer style.

I need not follow the circumlocution of legal phraseology. Suffice it to say, that there were several counts in his indictment.

I was first accused of having endeavoured to instigate to mutiny and revolt the slaves of the plantation Besançon, by having interfered to prevent one of their number from receiving his *just* punishment! Secondly, I had caused another of these to strike down his overseer; and afterwards had induced him to run away to the woods, and aided him in so doing! This was the slave Gabriel, who had just that day been captured in my company. Thirdly, and Gayarre now came to the cream of his accusation.

"Thirdly," continued he, "I accuse this person of having entered my house on the night of October the 18th, and having stolen therefrom the female slave Aurore Besançon."

"It is false!" cried a voice, interrupting him. "It is false! *Aurore Besançon is not a slave!*"

Gayarre started, as though some one had thrust a knife into him.

"Who says that?" he demanded, though with a voice that evidently faltered.

"I!" replied the voice; and at the same instant a young man leaped upon one of the benches, and stood with his head overtopping the crowd. It was D'Hauteville!

"I say it!" he repeated in the same firm tone. "*Aurore Besançon is no slave, but a free quadroon!* Here, Justice Claiborne," continued D'Hauteville, "do me the favour to read this document!" At the same time the speaker handed a folded parchment across the room.

The sheriff passed it to the magistrate, who opened it and read aloud.

It proved to be the "free papers" of Aurore the quadroon—the certificate of her manumission—regularly signed and attested by her master, Auguste Besançon, and left by him in his will.

The astonishment was extreme—so much so that the crowd seemed petrified, and preserved silence. Their feelings were on the turn.

The effect produced upon Gayarre was visible to all. He seemed covered with confusion. In his embarrassment he faltered out—

"I protest against this—that paper has been stolen from my bureau, and——

"So much the better, Monsieur Gayarre!" said D'Hauteville, again interrupting him; "so much the better! You confess to its being stolen, and therefore you confess to its being genuine. Now, sir; having this document in your possession, and knowing its contents, how could you claim Aurore Besançon as your slave?"

Gayarre was confounded. His cadaverous face became of a white sickly hue; and his habitual look of malice rapidly gave way to an expression of terror. He appeared as if he wanted to be gone; and already crouched behind the taller men who stood around him.

"Stop, Monsieur Gayarre!" continued the inexorable D'Hauteville, "I have not done with you yet. Here, Justice Claiborne! I have another document that may interest you. Will you have the goodness to give it your attention?"

Saying this, the speaker held out a second folded parchment, which was handed to the magistrate—who, as before, opened the document and read it aloud.

This was a codicil to the will of Auguste Besançon; by which the sum of fifty thousand dollars in bank stock was bequeathed to his daughter, Eugénie Besançon, to be paid to her upon the day on which she should be of age by the joint executors of the estate—M. Dominique Gayarre and Antoine Lereux—and these executors were instructed not to make known to the recipient the existence of this sum in her favour, until the very day of its payment.

"Now, Monsieur Dominique Gayarre!" continued D'Hauteville, as soon as the reading was finished, "I charge you with the embezzlement of this fifty thousand dollars, with various other sums—of which more hereafter. I charge you with having concealed the existence of this money—of having withheld it from the assets of the estate Besançon—of having appropriated it to your own use!"

"This is a serious charge," said Justice Claiborne, evidently impressed with its truth, and prepared to entertain it. "Your name, sir, if you please?" continued he, interrogating D'Hauteville, in a mild tone of voice.

It was the first time I had seen D'Hauteville in the full light of day. All that had yet passed between us had taken place either in the darkness of night, or by the light of lamps. That morning alone had we been together for a few minutes by daylight; but even then, it was under the sombre shadow of the woods—where I could have but a faint view of his features.

Now that he stood in the light of the open window, I had a full clear view of his face. The resemblance to some one I had seen before again impressed me. It grew stronger as I gazed; and, before the magistrate's interrogatory had received its reply, the shock of my astonishment had passed.

"Your name, sir, if you please?" repeated the justice.

"*Eugénie Besançon!*"

At the same instant the hat was pulled off—the black curls were drawn aside—and the fair golden tresses of the beautiful Creole exhibited to the view!

A loud huzza broke out—in which all joined, excepting Gayarre and his two or three ruffian adherents. I felt that I was free.

The conditions had suddenly changed, and the plaintiff had taken the place of the defendant. Even before the excitement had quieted down, I saw the sheriff, at the instigation of Reigart and others, stride forward to Gayarre; and, placing his hand upon the shoulder of the latter, arrest him as his prisoner.

"It is false!" cried Gayarre; "a plot—a damnable plot! These documents are forgeries! the signatures are false—false!"

"Not so, M. Gayarre," said the justice, interrupting him. "These documents are not forgeries. This is the handwriting of Auguste Besançon. I knew him well. This is his signature—I could myself swear to it."

"And I!" responded a voice, in a deep solemn tone, which drew the attention of all.

The transformation of Eugène D'Hauteville to Eugénie Besançon had astonished the crowd; but a greater surprise awaited them in the resurrection of the *steward Antoine!*

* * * * *

Reader! my story is ended. Here upon our little drama must the curtain drop. I might offer you other tableaux to illustrate the after history of our characters, but a slight summary must suffice. Your fancy will supply the details.

It will glad you to know, then, that Eugénie Besançon recovered the whole of her property—which was soon restored to its flourishing condition under the faithful stewardship of Antoine.

Alas! there was that that could never be restored—the young cheerful heart—the buoyant spirit—the virgin love!

But do not imagine that Eugénie Besançon yielded to despair—that she was ever after the victim of that unhappy passion. No—hers was a mighty will; and all its energies were employed to pluck the fatal arrow from her heart.

Time and a virtuous life have much power; but far more effective was that sympathy of the object beloved—that *pity for love*—which to her was fully accorded.

Her heart's young hope was crushed—her gay spirit shrouded—but there are other joys in life besides the play of the passions; and, it may be, the path of love is not the true road to happiness. Oh! that I could believe this! Oh! that I could reason myself into the belief, that that calm and unruffled mien—that soft sweet smile were the tokens of a heart at rest. Alas! I cannot. Fate will have its victims. Poor Eugénie! God be merciful to thee! Oh, that I could steep thy heart in the waters of Lethe!

And Reigart? You, reader, will be glad to know that the good doctor prospered—prospered until he was enabled to lay aside his lancet, and become a grandee planter—nay, more, a distinguished legislator,—one of those to whom belongs the credit of having modelled the present system of Louisiana law—the most advanced code in the civilised world.

You will be glad to learn that Scipio, with his Chloe and the "leetle Chloe," were brought back to their old and now happy home—that the snake-charmer still retained his brawny arms, and never afterwards had occasion to seek refuge in his tree-cavern.

You will not be grieved to know, that Gayarre passed several years of his after-life in the palace-prison of Baton Rouge, and then disappeared altogether from the scene. It was said that under a changed name he returned to France, his native country. His conviction was easy. Antoine had long suspected him of a design to plunder their joint ward, and had determined to put him to the proof. The raft of chairs had floated after all; and by the help of these the faithful steward had gained the shore, far down the river. No one knew of his escape; and the idea occurred to this strange old man to remain for a while *en perdu*—a silent spectator of the conduct of M. Dominique. No sooner did Gayarre believe him gone, than the latter advanced boldly upon his purpose, and hurried events to the described crisis. It was just what Antoine had expected; and acting himself as the accuser, the conviction of the avocat was easy and certain. A sentence of five years to the State Penitentiary wound up Gayarre's connexion with the characters of our story.

It will scarce grieve you to know that "Bully Bill" experienced a somewhat similar fate—that Ruffin, the man-hunter, was drowned by a sudden rising of the swamp—and that the "nigger-trader" afterwards became a "nigger-stealer;" and for that crime was sentenced at the court of Judge Lynch to the punishment of "tar and feathers."

The "sportsmen," Chorley and Hatcher, I never saw again—though their future is not unknown to me. Chorley—the brave and accomplished, but wicked Chorley—was killed in a duel by a Creole of New Orleans, with whom he had quarrelled at play.

Hatcher's bank "got broke" soon after; and a series of ill-fortune at length reduced him to the condition of a race-course thimble-rig, and small sharper in general.

The pork-merchant I met many years afterward, as a successful *monté* dealer in the "Halls of the Montezumas." Thither he had gone,—a camp-follower of the American army—and had accumulated an enormous fortune by keeping a gambling-table for the officers. He did not live long to enjoy his evil gains. The "*vomito prieto*" caught him at Vera Cruz; and his dust is now mingled with the sands of that dreary shore.

Thus, reader, it has been my happy fortune to record *poetical justice* to the various characters that have figured in the pages of our history.

I hear you exclaim, that two have been forgotten,—the hero and heroine?

Ah! no—not forgotten. Would you have me paint the ceremony — the pomp and splendour—the ribbons and rosettes—the after-scenes of perfect bliss?

Hymen, forbid! All these must be left to your fancy, if your fancy deign to act. But the interest of a " lover's adventures" usually ends with the consummation of his hopes — not even always extending to the altar — and you, reader, will scarce be curious to lift the curtain, that veils the tranquil after-life of myself and my beautiful

QUADROON.*

* See last Note in Appendix.

EXPLANATORY NOTES.

NOTES TO VOL. I.

"Father of Waters."—Page 1.

A poetic appellation of the Mississippi—an Indian idea. The word Mississippi itself is an Indian (Chipewa and Cree) compound of "misi" or "mitchi" great, and "sipi" river.

"Land of a thousand lakes."—Page 2.

Not *one* thousand, but *ten* thousand lakes may be enumerated in the region in which the Mississippi heads. This district is termed by Canadian voyageurs "Hauteur de terre," and by Americans "the Height of land," on account of its superior elevation to the surrounding country. There is nothing that deserves the name of mountain. The "Hauteur de terre" is only a portion of the great water-shed that divides the Hudson's Bay river system from that of the Mississippi Valley. Lake Itasca—the source of the "Father of Waters,"—is only 1400 feet above the sea, and *from* the sea by the windings of the river just 3160 miles. The fall of the Mississippi current from Itasca to its junction with the Missouri, averages 10 inches to the mile. From Missouri to the Belize, only 2½. If the Missouri be taken as the parent source of the Mississippi, the length of the great river must then be given as 4200 miles, making it by far the longest river in the world. At the Navy Yard, Memphis, Tennessee, it has been ascertained by observation, that the quantity of water annually passing through the channel of the Mississippi at that place was sufficient to cover an area of 100,000 square miles to the depth of seven and a half feet! Also, that the amount of silt it carried down would make a bed of earth one mile square and seventy-six feet deep! The current at this place was ascertained to be three miles per hour in the centre of the stream, though a little less at the sides. The Mississippi drains the entire space between the Alleghany and Rocky Mountain Chains, its "valley" thus embracing thirty degrees of longitude. In latitude it covers more than twenty degrees. Well may it be called the mighty river—the "Father of Waters."

"*Giant Moose.*"—Page 2.

The "moose" (*Cervus alces*) is the "elk" of Europe. The "wapiti" or "American elk" (*Cervus Canadensis*), is a very different animal, more resembling the red-deer of Europe. Both moose and wapiti are indigenous to the region around the sources of the Mississippi, which is not far from the southern limit of the range of the former.

"*Laugh of the wa-wa goose.*"—Page 3.

The "cacawee" (*Anas glacialis*) is so called by the voyageurs, from the note to which it gives utterance resembling these syllables. It has other trivial names in different parts, as "old wife," "old squaw," and "south southerly." The note of this species is often heard in the long winter nights of "Rupert's land," and forms the burden of many a voyageur song. The "wa-wa" goose is also named from its note, which the Indian hunter imitates by a prolonged utterance of the syllable "wah," while he at the same time strikes his lips with open palm, causing the repetition "wa-wa." Thus the goose is decoyed within shot. The trumpeter swan (*Cygnus buccinator*) also obtains its trivial name from the resemblance of its cry to the notes of a trumpet.

"*Rocks of St. Antoine.*"—Page 3.

The "Falls of St. Anthony"—the only cataract of the Mississippi—received their name from the earliest explorers, the French Jesuit Fathers. A town now stands near these falls, and settlements have been pushed into the wilderness much higher up.

"La montaigne qui trempe à l'eau."—Page 4.

"The mountain by the river side,"—the name of one of the many singular "bluffs" that form the characteristic scenery of the Upper Mississippi. "Pike's tent" is another, so called from the fact of Lieutenant Pike having first ascended it. Lake Pepin is a mere expansion of the river, forming a beautiful lake, about twenty-two miles in length. The "Lover's Leap" is a bold projecting rock elevated six hundred or seven hundred feet above the water. The Indian tradition relating to it is well known. Some fifty years ago, a beautiful Indian girl, the daughter of a chief, threw herself from its summit, in presence of the whole tribe, to avoid being united to a man whom her father had decided upon making her husband, and whom she was determined not to marry.

The "Cornice Rock" is another well-known landmark, deriving its name from the peculiar cornice-like formation of the rocks that here overhang the river.

"The aërial tomb of the adventurous miner."—
Page 5.

"Dubuque's Grave," another of these high bluffs, is a place of great notoriety, on the Upper Mississippi. It was the residence of the first mining pioneer of these regions, who held his title under a grant from the Mexican Government before the United States had extended its authority over the Louisiana territory. On the pinnacle of the bluff Dubuque erected his own tomb, and placed over it a cross and inscription. After his death, at his own request, his body was placed in this tomb upon a large flat stone, and here lay in state in its winding-sheet, exposed to the gaze of every traveller who might take the trouble of climbing to the summit of the bluff. The windows of the tomb are protected by iron gratings, through which the bones of the miner may still be seen mouldering where they were laid.

"*Golden tribute.*"—Page 6.

The colour of the Missouri is yellow. This colour it derives from one of its largest tributaries,—the "Yellow Stone." Below the influx of the Missouri, the waters of the Mississippi are changed to the hue of its "mighty brother."

"*Huge mounds.*"—Page 6.

The noted "Indian mounds" of St. Louis stand conspicuously near the bank of the river.

"*Famed river of the plains.*"—Page 7.

The Arkansas is, *par excellence*, the river of the prairies. It traverses a prairie country throughout its whole course.

"*Terraced groves.*"—Page 7.

These "terraced groves" of the Mississippi are one of the peculiarities of the scenery of the great river. They are caused by a peculiar process of formation. At some particular bend of the river, a new strip of soil is added each year by the deposit of the silt. Upon this the seed of the cottonwood (*Populus angulata*) is cast by the wind, and a crop of young trees springs up just as in a nursery. When these have attained a year's growth, another strip of *alluvion* becomes exposed, which receives a fresh shower of seed, and produces a fresher and younger growth of the trees. This process goes on for a series of years, until a regular terrace-like formation rises along one side of the river, while upon the opposite bank may be viewed the ancient forest, with the soil becoming regularly degraded, and the tall trees falling one after another into the whirling flood.

The light green colour of the cottonwood, especially when the tree is young, renders it a beautiful ornament to the scenery of the shores.

"*Cyprieres.*"—Page 8.

The immense cypress-forests of Louisiana are so called by the Creoles—in Anglo-American phraseology, "cypress-swamps."

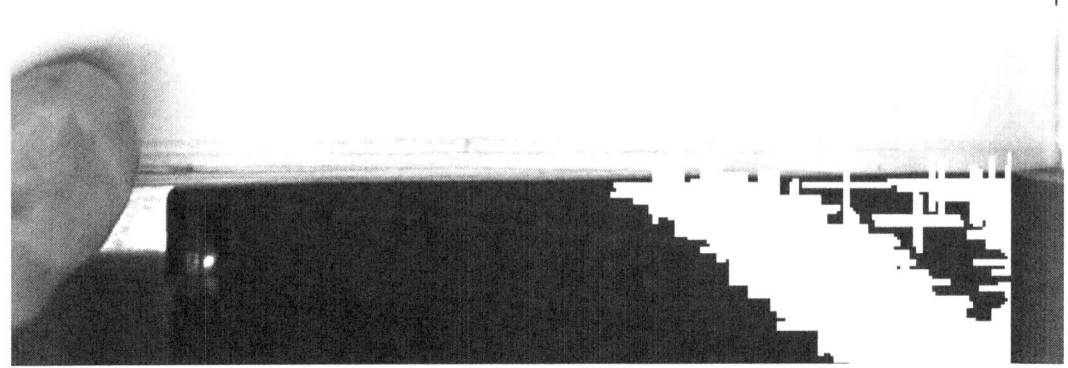

"*Sabal palm.*"—Page 9.

There are several species of these curious vegetable productions along the Southern belt of the old United States territory; viz. Florida, the Carolinas, and Louisiana. They have lately been removed from the genus *Chamærops*, and classed under that of *Sabal*. They are the most northerly representatives of the palms in the New world, as *Chamærops* is in the Old. The sabals are *fan-palms;* but it is curious that the most southern palms in America belong to species with pinnated leaves. The sabals of Louisiana are termed " Lataniers " by the French or Creole population, while the name " Palmetto " is that applied to them by the Anglo-Americans. They grow luxuriantly along the limit of the annual inundations, and in many places form dense thickets. Their presence denotes a rich soil, which is known as " palmetto land." From their tough fronds a fibre is obtained, which is much used in the manufacture of " palmetto hats," worn by the negroes and the poorer class of people, and very similar to those woven out of the fan-palm of Cuba.

"*Babylonian willow.*"—Page 9.

The " *Salix Babylonica* " and its kindred species, the weeping willow of America, are much cultivated as ornamental trees along the Lower Mississippi, and

its extensive trade in iron ware. Cincinnati, the "Queen City;" Louisville, the "Fall City;" New York, the "Empire City," &c. &c.

St. Louis is called "the Mound City," on account of the ancient mounds which exist in its neighbourhood.

"*Rowdy.*"—Page 27.

"Rowdy," an idle, rough, dissipated fellow—the American synonyme of the English "rough."

"*Levee of New Orleans.*"—Page 28.

The artificial dike or embankment of the Mississippi is termed the Levee. It is a French phrase from *lever*, to raise. This dike runs more than a hundred miles along the river. Of course, in front of the city of New Orleans, it is strongly built, and comprises the wharves or landing-places both for ships, flat boats, and steamers. All the river front is known by the general term "Levee," as in London we say "The Docks;" but when it is necessary to specify any particular portion of it, the "landing" is mentioned as, "Steamboat landing," "Ship landing," "Schooner landing," &c. &c.

The Levee dike is not unfrequently broken by

"*Blue cottonade.*"—Page 30.

This fabric is of cotton, woven by hand-looms, and generally manufactured by the poorer classes of Creoles throughout the settlements of Attakapas. It is usually dyed of a beautiful sky-blue fast colour, and at the time of which I am writing formed the material worn by half the population of Louisiana.

"*Boiler-burstings.*"—Page 34.

These occurrences are really frequent upon the American rivers, particularly the rivers of the West, where the boats are constructed for "high-pressure," and are consequently of a different build from sea-steamers. From twenty to fifty such accidents or catastrophes occur every year.

"*One state-room.*"—Page 37.

The little sleeping apartments in American steamboats are called "state-rooms." Each contains two beds or berths, and each has two doors—one leading into the main saloon, the other on the opposite side opening out upon the terrace-like guardway. There are some thirty or forty of these state-rooms in a Mississippi boat; and the accommodation thus afforded contrasts strongly with the filthy herding together which one experiences in a European steamer.

"*Landing.*"—Page 38.

Points upon the river-bank where boats may discharge freights are called "landings."

"*Drays.*"—Page 38.

Drays are numerous in New Orleans. The bales of cotton, hogsheads, &c., are all transported—or, as it is termed, "hauled"—upon drays.

"*Creole of twenty.*"—Page 44.

Creole and Quadroon girls often become women and mothers at the age of twelve—some even earlier! The same observation applies to the Spanish-American Creoles of Mexico and South America.

"*A Creole.*"—Page 45.

"Creole" is a term often misunderstood, even by Anglo-Americans. Some suppose that a Creole is a person of mixed blood. Not so. The Creole is the descendant of French parents *born in America*. The synonyme "Criollo" is used throughout all Spanish America to distinguish people of Spanish race, but of American birth, from Spaniards of old Spain. The French "Creole" and the Spanish "Criollo" bear respectively the same sort of relationship to a Frenchman and a Spaniard that a Yankee bears to an Englishman. "Creole" and "Criollo" signify "native." But the true Creole is not of mixed race—that is, not mixed as regards Indian or African descent. A Creole of mixed blood is termed "Creole mulatto," "Creole mestizo," "Creole quadroon," &c.; but never simply "Creole."

"*Can't-get-away.*"—Page 51.

There is a club in New Orleans called the "Can't-get-away Club," composed of gentlemen whose business occupations will not allow them to leave the city during the season of the epidemic.

"*Old boatman's song.*"—Page 52.

This may frequently be heard from the fore-deck of the Mississippi steam-boat; and the voices of the men, swelling over the broad bosom of the river, produce a fine effect. I remember on many occasions having been deeply impressed with this "boatman's chorus."

"*Lafayette and Carrolton.*"—Page 52.

Suburbs of New Orleans, above the city.

"*Dome of St. Charles.*"—Page 52.

St. Charles is a hotel, but such a hotel as is to be met with only in the United States. Its fine dome is the most striking feature in the aspect of New Orleans.

"*Floating palace.*"—Page 52.

This name is very commonly and very justly applied by Americans to their incomparable steamboats.

"*Hurricane deck.*"—Page 60.

The roof which covers the cabin of a Mississippi steam-boat affords a fine promenade. It is covered with canvas, and seats are usually provided upon it. There a cool breeze may always be obtained when the boat is in motion. In windy weather a "hurricane" may be expected upon it,—hence its name.

"*The silent pilot.*"—Page 60.

The "man at the wheel" of an American steamer is not stationed on the poop as upon sea-going vessels. His wheel is placed within a little glass house, upon the most prominent point of the roof, far forward, so that he commands a perfect view of his course.

"*Bayous.*"—Page 63.

The "bayou" is peculiar to Louisiana. The word is of Spanish origin, and denotes a sluggish stream. It is scarcely synonymous with the American word "creek," which means a stream smaller than a "river." The bayous have a peculiarity which characterises them, viz., at different seasons of the year they change their current and run backwards. This peculiarity is caused by the annual inundations. Some hundreds of streams in Louisiana are called "bayous."

"*Coasts.*"—Page 63.

The shores of the Lower Mississippi are termed "Coasts" in the language of the country. Some portions have specific names, as the "German Coast," which was settled at an early period by a colony of Germans; the "Acadian Coast," because peopled by emigrants from Canada (Acadia); the "French Coast," &c. &c. The appellation of Coast is not used on the upper portions of the Mississippi. The "Coast" of the Mississippi is the "bogey" of the Tennessee, or Kentucky slave. When a negro of these parts gives offence to his master, a common mode of terrifying him is to tell him he will be sold upon the Coast —that is, consigned to the severe work and cruel treatment experienced upon the large sugar-plantations.

"*Top of a ridge.*"—Page 64.

This running along the top of a ridge is only apparent. When it is remembered that the Mississippi is at this place over 150 feet in depth, it will be perceived that its bed is by far the lowest valley in the country through which it passes.

"*Dark forest.*"—Page 64.

The indigenous *sylva* of Louisiana is comprised in the following genera: *Cupressus, Diospyros, Fagus, Magnolia, Liriodendron, Liquidambar, Fraxinus, Laurus, Juniperus, Juglans, Gleditschia, Morus, Populus, Pinus, Nyssa, Pavia, Platanus, Quercus, Vitis, Vaccineum, Sambucus, Ulmus, Robinia, Tilia, Rubus, Cornus, Celtis, Sabal, Arundo, Acer; Asimina, Bignonia, Carpinus, Cerasus, Castanea, Betula,* and *Andromeda*. Many of these genera are represented by several species, as the oak, the maple, *Juglans,* and *Magnolia;* while others have but one species within the limits of Louisiana, as *Platanus, Populus, Ilex, Liriodendron, Diospyros,* &c.

"*Fête-champêtre.*"—Page 66.

The Creoles inherit all the *esprit* and gaiety which characterise their Gallic ancestry. They are a pleasure-loving people. The *fête-champêtre* is a common mode of amusement along the French coast of the Mississippi. Such re-unions are often upon a grand

and expensive scale. Balls, too, are of frequent occurrence. When one of these is to come off at any particular village or plantation along the "coast," a brace of horsemen set forth, one going up and the other down the river. Each of these is provided with a horn, which he blows in front of the houses in passing. At sound of the horn, a young Creole girl trips out upon the porch, shouting out the inquiry, "Where is it?" The place and the hour are all that is asked for. The rest is understood, and no special invitation is either given or expected.

"*Flat.*"—Page 70.

"Flat boats" are still extensively used upon the Mississippi and its tributaries. Of course they are only carried down-stream, as it would not repay the labour to row them back to their point of embarkation. They are used to convey large cargoes of corn, pork, &c., from the upper country, which can be in this way transported at less expense than by the steamboats. On arriving at New Orleans, their cargoes are sold, and the boats themselves disposed of for "lumber." The crews return to their homes upon the steamers.

"*A Creole fashion.*"—Page 75.

The fashion of wearing the hair, which is now termed *à la Eugénie,* was in vogue among the Creole women of Louisiana twenty years ago. The Empress is, therefore, only an imitator.

" 'Scape-pipe."—Page 81.

The steam "escapes" upon the high-pressure boats of the Mississippi through a pipe or funnel that stands up above the hurricane-deck. The size and power of the boat can be guessed at by the tone of the " 'scape-pipe." Although to the unpractised ear the reports of two boats of equal size sound alike, yet some old residents along the river can distinguish one from the other, and tell *what boat it is*, long before the vessel appears in sight.

" Hands."—Page 81.

The firemen and others employed on the boats are termed " deck-hands."

" Billets of cordwood."—Page 82.

The Mississippi boats use "cordwood,"—that is, billets cut into lengths of four feet each and six or eight inches in diameter. Upon the Upper Ohio, coal is employed occasionally, as it is there accessible.

" Burning bacon hams."—Page 86.

The burning of " bacon hams " to create a greater power of steam is no fancy of the author. Such a thing has frequently occurred upon the Mississippi river. "What a waste!" I hear one exclaim. That, however, is a misconception. When the wood has attained a certain high price, and the hams can be purchased for two cents per pound, there is no waste whatever. It is a question of economy not well understood by the million. There is no waste in impelling steamboats by bacon hams, if these can be *produced with the same amount of human labour as* it requires to furnish the wood or coal.

"*Dug-out.*"—Page 87.

A phrase used in the West to designate an ill-made canoe—*i. e.* dug or rudely hollowed out from the trunk of a tree. It is here ironically employed.

"*Shute.*"—Page 95.

Where the Mississippi has cut out for itself a new channel, an island is formed, and the river then runs on both sides of the island. One of these passages is termed a "shute."

"*Baton Rouge.*"—Page 102.

"Baton Rouge" is a town, and one of the oldest settlements in Louisiana. It is the political capital of the State, and contains several fine public buildings, as the "State-house," "Penitentiary," &c.

"*A life-preserver.*"—Page 110.

Were it made compulsory on all travellers to carry the life-preserver, thousands of lives would be annually saved. But legislation disdains to adopt any means for the benefit of mankind. Most of the cares of Government are about measures antagonistic to the welfare of the people.

"*China-tree.*"—Page 128.

The "pride of China," or "China-tree," as it is called in Louisiana, is the Indian lilac (*Melia azed arach*). It is a great favourite on the Lower Mississippi, where it is planted around the houses of the planters, and in the streets of the villages. The climate of Louisiana suits this noble tree, which there arrives at its full perfection of flower and foliage.

"*Brogans.*"—Page 131.

A sort of jack boots worn by the negroes is so called. A finer sort, also termed "brogans," is seen upon planters and others.

"*Jeans.*"—Page 131.

The home-made cloth denominated "jeans" is the principal material with which the slaves are clothed. A very coarse article, woven of inferior cotton, and dyed a copper colour with the bark of the catalpa-tree, is in use for slave-shirts and blouses.

"*Scipio Besançon.*"—Page 133.

The slave usually takes the patronymic of his master.

"*Donicks.*"—Page 143.

Pebbles or paving-stones. A western appellation of unknown origin.

"*Planters' bank.*"—Page 144.

The name of a bank well known in the south-west.

"*Boss.*"—Page 146.

"Boss," master. So the negroes address all white men having authority over them. At the Cape of Good Hope, the Dutch "Baas" is similarly employed, and would seem to be the root or synonyme of the American "Boss."

"*A Quadroon.*"—Page 165.

The progeny of a mulatto mother and a white father — often as white as the male parent himself, but not the less doomed to the accursed destiny of the slave mother. Many of the quadroons of New Orleans are the most beautiful women in the place. In this respect they are quite as distinguished as the Creole ladies, who are themselves justly distinguished for great personal beauty.

"*Georgian peach.*"—Page 168.

Georgian peach,—a fine variety of the peach, noted for its beautiful carmine-red bloom.

"*Roasted opossum.*" Page 185.

Excellent eating is the opossum (*Didelphis Virginiana*). The flesh of this animal tastes very much like young " roast pig." The " 'coon," however, is quite a different affair, though the negroes eat this " varmint " readily.

"*A keel.*"—Page 192.

The " keel " boat is frequently seen upon the Western waters. This craft is usually employed by traders, who call with their merchandise at the various settlements along the rivers. The keel is not abandoned in New Orleans like the " flat." The former is too valuable to be broken up, but is taken up the river again and laden for a new voyage. Keels are usually towed up-stream by the smaller steamboats.

"*Ruby throat.*"—Page 193.

Humming-bird (*Trochilus Coluber*), the only species, with one other exception, that is known to migrate within the limits of the United States.

"*Cowskin.*"—Page 196.

"Cowskin," or "cowhide," the name of the whip in general use throughout the Mississippi Valley. They are twisted from raw-hide, about four feet in length, and usually painted red or blue.

"*Ugly corpse I'll make.*"—Page 201.

Literally true.

"*Mike Fink.*"—Page 201.

The name of one of the most notorious of the Mississippi boatmen—a man who has left behind him the reputation of having "one virtue and a thousand crimes."

"*Passes.*"—Page 204.

It is the custom in the Slave States to give written permission to the slaves when they leave the limits of the plantation—even upon the shortest errand.

"*Nigger-driver.*"—Page 209.

A spiteful appellation used by the slaves when speaking of their overseers.

"*Its billiard salon.*"—Page 226.

The Creoles are fine billiard-players; some of them the most expert—perhaps in the world. Indeed billiard-playing is much more practised in the United States than in any part of Europe.

"*Sangaree.*"—Page 239.

Composed of claret, iced water, and sugar, with a sprinkle of nutmeg. A favourite drink in the Southern States.

"*African blood.*"—Page 267.

This *fraud upon the laws of Louisiana* was actually practised by a young German, who wished to marry a Quadroon girl, and settle in the country.

"*Purple martin.*"—Page 273.

The farmers of America provide little cots, or "martin-boxes," for these beautiful summer visitors; and almost every house has one. The negroes accomplish the same purpose, as described in the text. Before the time of either farmers or negroes, the simple Indians used to hang gourd-shells upon the branches of the trees around their encampment—thus securing the purple swallow for a semi-annual pet.

"*Pic.*"—Page 276.

The "picayune" and "bit" are the small silver coins in circulation in the South-West. They are imported from the Spanish-American States, particularly Mexico. The picayune is the Mexican "medio," worth $6\frac{1}{4}$ cents. The bit is the real of just double this value. The "dime," of ten cents value, is the legal American coin, but it requires strong measures to give circulation to a new currency.

"*Porch.*"—Page 277.

It is considered a house of some pretensions, when a porch or portico is added.

"*Chopping.*"—Page 278.

The Western phrase for wood-cutting with an axe.

"*Fleur-de-lis.*"—Page 283.

Under the old French code of Louisiana branding with the fleur-de-lis was one of the modes of punishing the slave. Some of the old "brands" may yet be seen among the plantation negroes.

"*Concealed weapons.*"—Page 305.

The statement here made is no exaggeration. Even "men of peace" went armed at the time I speak of, and thousands in the Mississippi Valley still follow the fashion.

NOTES TO VOL. II.

"Loungers of the bar."—Page 8.

The room appropriated to the guests of an American village hotel, where they assemble to await the hour of meals, has usually a drinking-bar on one side; hence the name of "bar" given to the whole apartment.

"Raccoon."—Page 9.

Naturalists allege that the raccoon (*Procyon lotor*) is nocturnal in his habits. This is but partially true. I have observed this animal in dark shady woods, following his predatory game by day. The raccoon, like many other animals, has probably been driven to nocturnal prowling through fear of the hunter, his most dreaded enemy. The singular habit of this creature to plunge his food into the water before devouring it is well known. The opossum is also often seen by day in the American woods.

"Swamp hare."—Page 9.

The "swamp hare" (*Lepus aquaticus*), or "swamp rabbit," as it is often called, is one of the largest of

American hares. In size it is equal to the Irish hare, but far inferior to the latter in swiftness, and yields but poor sport to the hunter. It is only found in the southern part of the United States, and, as its name implies, is a denizen of the vast marsh-tracts of that region.

"*Metallic plumage.*"—Page 10.

The beautiful sheen of the wild turkey—the male bird—can scarcely be appreciated by those who have only observed the mounted specimens in a museum. A rich metallic lustre glosses the whole plumage, which fades to a certain extent after life is extinct. The turkey is one of those species that does not increase in size under domestication. The wild bird is considerably larger than the "gobbler" of the farm-yard. The Honduras turkey, whose plumage almost rivals the peacock, does not range so far north as the United States territory. It is strictly a bird of the tropical forests.

"*Cotton-rose.*"—Page 11.

The wild "althea," or "cotton-rose," of Louisiana, is the *Hibiscus grandiflorus*. Its leaves resemble large strawberry-leaves, and its corolla, of five inches diameter, bears a resemblance to a wild rose; hence the trivial appellation of "cotton-rose."

"*Large liliaceous blossoms.*"—Page 12.

There is a peculiarity about the efflorescence of the *Magnolia grandiflora* that deserves mention. It commences flowering in May, and continues to produce fresh blossoms throughout the whole summer, so that, like the orange, its fruit and flowers may be seen growing together upon the same tree. The *Magnolia glauca* possesses a similar property when growing in moist ground; but it is not so with any of the other American magnolias.

Nothing can excel the perfume of the magnolia in sweetness, though the odour is esteemed "sickening" by some persons. It is a strange fact that, though the magnolias are decidedly trees of a sub-tropical climate, no species of them is indigenous to South Europe, Africa, or South America. Their range is very limited in North America, and also in the Himalayas. According to Dr. Hooker, magnolia forests in the Himalayas are more extensive than in any part of the United States; but this botanist is speaking of the true magnolias. Regarding the liriodendron, or tulip-tree, as a magnolia, its range in North America is very extensive, and large tracts of *poplar* forests—so the tree is called—exist in most of the southern and middle States.

"*Sassafras laurel.*"—Page 12.

The *Laurus sassafras* is one of the most interesting trees of America. The peculiar pale green colour of its leaves renders it conspicuous amidst the other trees. A decoction of its roots is extensively used, during the spring season, as a blood-purifier, and the inhabitants of the Mississippi Valley have much belief in its medicinal virtues. In Louisiana its leaves are used to thicken pottage, and in Virginia a beer is made of the young shoots. But, perhaps, the most interesting fact in relation to this tree is, that it may be said to have led to the discovery of America, as it was its strong fragrance smelt by Columbus that encouraged him to persevere when his crew mutinied, and enabled him to convince them that land was near at hand.

The *Laurus sassafras* is found throughout most part of the United States, and extends into Mexico, and even to South America.

"*The sumach.*"—Page 12.

Every one has heard of the glowing colours of the American forest in autumn. There are many trees which combine to produce these brilliant tints. The *rhus*, or sumach, is one of the most conspicuous. The leaves of the species known as "stag's-horn sumach" (*Rhus typhina*) turn, before dropping off, to a purplish and yellowish red; and the "poison sumach" (*Rhus venenata*) presents a still more brilliant blending of scarlet and purple.

The tupelo (*Nyssa*), particularly the *Nyssa candicans*, or ogechœ lime-tree, also presents a beautiful aspect in autumn,—both leaves and fruit being of bright scarlet. Several species of *Acer* — among others, the sugar-maple—also turn scarlet; and the American beech, particularly where it grows as an underwood, may be seen of a beautiful gold and translucent yellow.

Many other species contribute to produce the variegated hues of an American forest.

"*Crotalus.*"—Page 24.

This is a fact in relation to the rattlesnake. The bite is certain to prove fatal during the hot months of autumn, if an antidote is not used. Cases of death from the bite of the rattlesnake are rare; but this is accounted for by the fact that few persons are bitten by these serpents, and also that there are several species of crotalus more or less venomous. The bite of the most dangerous of the tribe *Crotalus horridus*, or *durissus*, certainly produces death, and in the short period mentioned.

"*Tillandsia.*"—Page 25.

The *Tillandsia usneoides*, or "Spanish moss," as it is called in the Southern States, is one of the most singular parasites in the world. It has been called "old man's beard," from its resemblance to hoary hair. It hangs down from the branches in long straggling masses, frequently reaching to the surface of the earth. Sometimes a whole forest of cypresses, live oaks, or cotton-woods, is thickly tangled with it, and the sun's rays completely shrouded from the sight.

The tillandsia is used throughout the Southern States for stuffing sofas, mattrasses, cushions, &c.; and, when carefully picked and dried, is not much inferior to the best curled hair.

"*The Bambarra.*"—Page 38.

Of all the African races that have been carried into the New world, those of the Bambarra tribe are the most fierce and turbulent in their disposition. In Cuba, where many of these people have been imported, they are regarded as the most dangerous of the negro population.

"*Stung me unprovoked.*"—Page 41.

The rattlesnake rarely strikes without being offended or trodden upon. It will retreat if not molested, but there is little danger in a conflict with one, as they are the most sluggish of the serpent tribe. Boys in the backwoods will venture to approach a rattlesnake, and kill it with a stick or sapling.

"*Eight feet in length.*"—Page 63.

The " crotalus " is rarely found more than four

feet long, though rare specimens occur of double that length.

"*Serpents of the genus Constrictor.*"—Page 64.

The "black snake" of America (*Coluber constrictor*), though not larger than the rattlesnake, will attack the latter; and from his superior power of "constriction" often succeeds in killing his dreaded antagonist. The black snake has no venomous fangs, but is much more active and powerful than serpents of the genus *crotalus*.

"*Aristolochia.*"—Page 67.

The "guaco," or "bejuco de guaco," is the plant so celebrated by the graceful pen of the Spanish botanist, Mutis. A species of hawk that lives chiefly on serpents, when about to attack any of the venomous species, is known to eat the leaves of this plant. The observation of this by the natives of South America led to the discovery of the antidote, and among the Indians and Negroes of New Granada "snake-charmers" are common enough. They rely upon this plant to protect them from the serpent venom. Some inoculate themselves with its juice by means of incisions made between their toes and fingers, and over other parts of the body. Thus prepared, the bite of the most venomous serpents—such as the lance-headed viper (*V. trigonocephalus*), the "coral snake," and the "dangerous bushmaster,"—is no longer dreaded.

The "guaco" obtains its trivial name from the note of the "guaco bird," which resembles the syllables "gua-co gua-co," rapidly repeated.

"*Tracked by hounds.*"—Page 70.

It will hardly be credited that such a practice exists in the Southern States of civilised America. Such, however, is unfortunately the fact, as might be easily shown. Indeed a report of negro-hunting by dogs is no uncommon thing in the pages of the public newspapers.

"*Eat snake.*"—Page 71.

The flesh of the rattlesnake is not unpalatable, as I have been assured by those who have eaten of it. The head is usually cut off as soon as the reptile is killed—though that is by no means necessary to ensure safety to the snake-eater, since serpent-poison taken into the stomach is perfectly innocuous.

"*Knees.*"—Page 78.

The cypress "knees" form one of the most curious puzzles in the vegetable world. These monstrosities rise around the base of the tree, at some distance from the trunk, and sometimes attain a height of several feet. They are ligneous, like the trunk itself, but never send forth shoots or suckers. They are always hollow within, with a smooth reddish bark, and soft wood resembling that of the roots upon which they grow. They are conical in form. No cause can be assigned for their existence. They are peculiar to the *Taxodium*, and begin to appear when the tree is only twenty feet high. The negroes make use of them for bee-hives.

The "buttock" of the cypress is equally curious. This is often many yards in circumference, and its surface is furrowed by longitudinal channels that run tortuously up the trunk. The "buttock" itself is usually hollow, and on account of its worthlessness as timber, the wood-cutters erect a scaffolding around the tree, and fell it at the height of several feet from the ground. A more common mode of felling the cypress is during the periods of inundation. Then no scaffold is required, as the water reaches up to the top of the buttock, and the wood-cutter can approach the real trunk in a skiff or pirogue which serves in place of the scaffolding otherwise used.

"*Chippewa.*"—Page 81.

The Chippewa Indians are the most expert of all the tribes in canoe management, as their birch-bark canoes are the most perfect models of watercraft. Some of the negroes of the Southern States, however, understand well the use of the paddle, though there the birchen canoe is not known. Its substitute is the "dug-out," or canoe hollowed out of a log —usually the trunk of the tulip-tree, or cottonwood.

"*Chunk.*"—Page 90.

"Chunk," a bulky piece of anything—an American phrase. "Pone"—a loaf of maize-bread of the size of a paving-stone, is so called by the Southern negroes.

"*Roastin' yeers.*"—Page 92.

The young heads of maize when boiled or roasted, make most delicious food. Either boiled or roasted they are termed "roasting ears."

"*Corn-cob with a piece of cane-joint.*"—Page 93.

The piece of cob is hollowed out and serves for the bowl of the pipe, while the cane-joint makes the shank. A pipe in common use among the "field hands" of the plantations.

"*A painter.*"—Page 98.

"Panther." The cougar (*Felis concolor*).

"*Killed the catamount.*"—Page 99.

It is astonishing the ignorance that exists among the American people in relation to the indigenous animals of their country, but indeed this ignorance is scarcely peculiar to Americans. The remark will apply to the people of every other land. The catamount is a name given to almost every sort of creature that is rarely seen—now to the cougar, now to the bay-lynx, and sometimes to the fisher and wolverene. The bay-lynx, however, is the animal chiefly pointed at by the appellation "catamount;" and although this creature would run from a child, rare powers are often ascribed to it.

"*Sacré Cœur.*"—Page 111.

The name of a celebrated and rich convent of nuns of New Orleans.

"*Uncle.*"—Page 126.

Old negroes are thus familiarly addressed by their white masters.

"*Houma or de Choctuma.*"—Page 127.

The names of two boats that formerly "ran" in the Red River trade. The names are taken from two Indian tribes of Louisiana—now nearly extinct.

"*A reality.*"—Page 139.

Only those who have witnessed the boldness and ferocity of the Norway rat, when in large numbers and hungered, can give credit to the adventure described. The author can assure the reader, there is truth in the incident. At the time of its occurrence the towns upon the Mississippi swarmed with Norway rats; and so predatory had they become, that it was found necessary to offer a bounty for their destruction. The night police were particularly charged with this duty, and in passing through the streets at midnight, you might see the watchman accompanied by a pair of stout rat dogs, carrying out his commission with great energy. The vast stores of cotton bales and lumber in New Orleans, as also its wooden wharves, ensured the rats a place of refuge; and in that climate of rank vegetation, these animals had multiplied exceedingly. Their numbers made them bold; and in passing through the streets on a moonlight night, you might see hundreds of them, running before your feet, and scarcely frightened by your presence.

"*South Sea.*"—Page 165.

Many of these hats known as "Panama hats," cost the enormous price of $125, or 25*l.* !

"*St. Charles or Verandah.*"—Page 170.

The two hotels in New Orleans most popular and noted for their excellent drinking " bars."

"*Down South.*"—Page 177.

To the inhabitant of the Western States, a trip to New Orleans is " down South."

"*Dog gone me!*"—Page 178.

" Dog gone," and " darn," are in Western phraseology common expressions. They are supposed to be a delicate substitute for the more English " damn."

"*Corn-shucks.*"—Page 186.

Corn-husks. The envelope of the ears of the maize. Its worthless nature explains its application as in the text.

"*Shinplasters.*"—Page 187.

The small bank-notes were thus jocularly styled.

"*Cottonade.*"—Page 195.

A beautiful and durable fabric, usually dyed a fast blue colour, which appears to grow fresher and brighter each time the garment is washed. It was woven by hand-looms, and was of excellent quality, but the "imitation article," produced by the mills of Massachusetts, has driven the better kind out of the market, and it is now rarely seen even in Louisiana.

"*Quadroon-balls*"—Page 214.

A species of balls peculiar to New Orleans, where the female dancers are quadroon or mulatto girls. Of course the gentlemen are white.

"*L'Abeille.*"—Page 219.

Several of the New Orleans journals are printed half in French and half in English. This is to accommodate both the French and American populations.

"*Swamp.*"—Page 243.

The "swamp" comes up close to the rear of the city of New Orleans. In fact, some streets extend to its very margin, and inundations, that lay the houses several feet under water, are not uncommon.

"*After death are drowned.*"—Page 243.

At eighteen inches below the surface water is reached, and of course fills the grave. Those who can afford it, deposit their dead in oven-like vaults. These are arranged in rows, but the hot sun shining down upon their mason-work, gives one the disagreeable idea that the tenants of these vaults must from day to day undergo a sort of baking process.

"*First municipality.*"—Page 253.

New Orleans is divided into three municipal governments, or "municipalities," as they are termed. Each having its own mayor and council. The *first municipality* is the old city or French quarter.

"*Butts of pistols.*"—Page 254.

The scene here described may be witnessed at the entrance of any ball-room in New Orleans, even at the present day.

NOTES TO VOL. III.

"*Tree-crickets.*"—Page 15.

Silence in the Louisiana forest during the summer season is a thing quite unknown. Both by night and day there is a constant humming, and chirping, and croaking, and squeaking, that almost drowns the voices of persons in conversation. The numerous species of frogs and tree-toads and *cicadae*, produce noisy medley.

"*Negro-trader.*"—Page 20.

One whose business is dealing in human beings—buying and selling men, women, and children. It is needless to say that such men have but a very indifferent character for morality.

"*Rotundo.*"—Page 21.

The "Rotundo," where the slaves are sold by public auction, is a large circular hall in the building of the St. Louis or "French exchange." The American or "St. Charles exchange" is in the St. Charles hotel.

"*Claret or blue.*"—Page 32.

The tailors of New Orleans are, perhaps, the best in the world. At the time of which I speak — some twenty years ago—it was no uncommon thing in New Orleans to be charged 20*l.* for a coat, but it *was* a coat—such an one as Brummel might have worn.

"*Pickery.*"—Page 33.

A place where the cotton is cleared of its seed or "picked." The name in New Orleans is applied to the smaller kinds of cotton-presses, such as are worked by hand-power or horses, in contradistinction to the steam-presses. The "cotton-press" requires a word of explanation. Two or three of the most conspicuous buildings in New Orleans are cotton-presses. These buildings are of immense size—one of them covering many acres of ground. They consist, however, of little more than walls and roof, to serve as a storage for the cotton. The mechanical department is simple enough: a small steam-engine, by the power of which the huge bales of cotton are compressed to little more than half the bulk, to which the small press of the planter has already reduced them. Of course, the object in thus lessening their size is to render them more fit for stowage in the holds of outward-bound ships.

"*Shad-bellied.*"—Page 33.

"Quaker-cut" is so called in the United States, on account of the slanting skirt bearing a fancied resemblance to the shape of the shad-fish.

"*Poked their fingers.*"—Page 34.

Literally true. A common circumstance at a negro sale.

"*Yellow girl.*"—Page 46.

Mulatto girls are called "yellow girls."

"*Toque.*"—Page 47.

The "toque" is the head-dress worn by the quadroon girls of Louisiana. It is also worn by mulattoes and blacks throughout all the Southern States and in the West Indies. Nothing in the shape of head-cover can be more becoming than this. It is even picturesque — much more so than the Oriental turban, than which it is lighter-looking and far cleaner. It is simply a square handkerchief of the species known as "Madras," folded around the head, and knotted in a peculiar style. There is more than one "fashion" of adjusting the toque; and among the wearers there is no little taste exhibited in this respect. The Madras kerchief which forms the toque is of different patterns—usually chequered—but the most beautiful are those of large plaid-like checks—combining the colours of crimson, green, white, and scarlet. Some of these kerchiefs cost as high as five pounds sterling, but their colours are fast, and they wear "for ever."

"*Coachmen of New Orleans.*"—Page 64.

Brigands, as elsewhere.

"*Mustangs.*"—Page 74.

From an early period, there has been a trade in horses, mules, and cattle from the Spanish settlements in Texas, " overland" to Louisiana; so that the small Andalusian horse is not uncommon in the South-western States. In the Atlantic States this race is never seen. The wild horses of the Texan prairies are called " musteños" by the Mexicans—by the Americans " mustangs." Tough active creatures are these mustangs, and

"Sweltering will gallop a long summer's day."

" *'Coon-hunter.*"—Page 82.

A moonlight night is always chosen for the 'coon-hunt.

"*Pawpaw thicket.*"—Page 88.

The pawpaw (*asimina*) rarely reaches twenty feet in height, and usually grows as an underwood in thick shaded forests. Its leaves are large and laurel-like, and its stem is soft and easily broken. There are several species of the pawpaw in the American woods, but the most common is the *Asimina triloba*. The fruit of the pawpaw is " eatable, but not worth eating." It is relished, however, by the negroes, who devour it greedily. The fruit is about three inches long, and half as much in thickness. It is of a yellow colour when ripe, and of an ovate oblong shape. It contains a yellow pulp of sweet luscious taste. All parts of the tree — leaves, bark, flowers, and fruit—have a rank, slightly fetid, and disagreeable smell. The leaves lie over each other in such a manner as to give a peculiar imbricated appearance to the whole plant. The flowers are campanulate and drooping.

"*Drive*."—Page 138.

A deer-hunt with hounds and horses is termed a "drive." "Standmen" are stationed at intervals across the line of the chase, and the game is driven upon them; hence the terms "driving" and "drive," as applied to the American deer-hunt.

"*Blaze*."—Page 145.

A piece of bark cut off with an axe is termed a blaze. It is the usual mode of marking out a path through the woods, and also the boundary lines between two proprietors.

"*Cord of wood*."—Page 146.

A cord of wood is a fixed quantity, and contains one hundred and twenty-eight cubic feet. It is computed by measurement. The wood-chopper cuts the billets to exactly four feet in length, and, building them in piles of four feet high and eight long, thus presents them in " cords," ready for sale.

"*Cobbing-board.*"—Page 171.

Another instrument for slave-torture. It is a piece of flat paddle-like board, with auger holes bored in it, to be laid upon the hips, thus inflicting painful strokes.

"*Blueskin.*"—Page 174.

A phrase sometimes used as a term of reproach to people of colour.

"*Skiffs.*"—Page 184.

Small boats without keels are so called in the Western States. These, and the "dug-out," or tree canoe, are the sort of craft in use upon the creeks, ponds, and rivers of the Mississippi Valley.

"*Posse.*"—Page 203.

Posse comitatus.

"*Squire.*"—Page 209.

Justices of the Peace in the States are always so designated.

"*Camp-follower.*"—Page 226.

This man was a Georgian by birth. He will be remembered by all who served in Scott's campaign in Mexico. He had accumulated $200,000 by gambling with the officers of the American army, and was returning with his money to the United States when he was taken by "Yellow Jack" at Vera Cruz, and died there.

NOTE TO THE PREFACE.

After what has been stated in the Preface, it will scarce be necessary to say that the *names* and some of the *places* mentioned in this book are fictitious. Some of the scenes, and many of the characters that figure in these pages, are *real*, and there are those living who will recognise them.

The book is "founded" upon an actual experience. It was written many years ago, and would have been then published, but for the interference of a well-known work, which treated of similar scenes and subjects. That work appeared just as the "Quadroon" was about to be put to the press; and the author of the latter, not willing to risk the chances of being considered an imitator, had determined on keeping the "Quadroon" from the public.

Circumstances have ruled it otherwise; and having rewritten some parts of the work, he now presents it to the reader as a painting—somewhat coarse and crude, perhaps—of life in Louisiana.

The author disclaims all "intention." The book has been written neither to aid the Abolitionist nor glorify the planter. The author does not believe that by such means he could benefit the slave, else he would not fear to avow it. On the other hand, he is too true a Republican, to be the instrument that would add one drop to the "bad blood" which, unfortunately for the cause of human freedom, has already arisen between "North" and "South." No; he will be the last man to aid European despots in this, their dearest wish and desperate hope.

London, July, 1856.

THE END.

London:—Printed by G. BARCLAY, Castle St. Leicester Sq.

CPSIA information can be obtained at www.ICGtesting.com
Printed in the USA
LVOW02s0003290714

396388LV00017B/649/P